Your Horoscope 2022

Leo

23 July – 23 August

igloobooks

igloobooks

Published in 2021
First published in the UK by Igloo Books Ltd
An imprint of Igloo Books Ltd
Cottage Farm, NN6 0BJ, UK
Owned by Bonnier Books
Sveavägen 56, Stockholm, Sweden
www.igloobooks.com

0721 001
2 4 6 8 10 9 7 5 3 1
ISBN 978-1-80022-524-4

Written by Belinda Campbell and Denise Evans

Designed by Simon Parker
Edited by Natalie Graham

Printed and manufactured in China

CONTENTS

INTRODUCTION

This 15-month guide has been designed and written to give a concise and accessible insight into both the nature of your star sign and the year ahead. Divided into two main sections, the first section of this guide will give you an overview of your character in order to help you understand how you think, perceive the world and interact with others and – perhaps just as importantly – why. You'll soon see that your zodiac sign is not just affected by a few stars in the sky, but by planets, elements and a whole host of other factors, too.

The second section of this guide is made up of daily forecasts. Use these to increase your awareness of what might appear on your horizon so that you're better equipped to deal with the days ahead. While this should never be used to dictate your life, it can be useful to see how your energies might be affected or influenced, which in turn can help you prepare for what life might throw your way.

By the end of these 15 months, these two sections should have given you a deeper understanding and awareness of yourself and, in turn, the world around you. There are never any definite certainties, but with an open mind you will find guidance for what might be, and learn to take more control of your own destiny.

THE CHARACTER OF THE LION

....

A fire sign ruled by the Sun was surely destined to always burn the brightest. Like a moth to a flame, people are naturally drawn to Leonians. Whether singing on a stage, dancing in a club or playing football in the park, they dominate every situation by demanding attention and adoration. Born in the fifth house in the zodiac calendar, which represents pleasure and creativity, Leonians often derive immense satisfaction and a sense of purpose from making others happy. These fiery lions can be brimming with confidence or struggle with a lack thereof, and need to be validated with constant praise. The laughter of others is like music to their ears and a career in comedy, like fellow Leonians David Walliams and Jo Brand, could be their calling.

Born in the middle of summer, Leo is a fixed sign that works hard at making dreams become a reality. Daring Leonians Amelia Earhart, Neil Armstrong and Barack Obama achieved historical firsts when realising their dreams. Courageous and not averse to taking risks, fortune definitely favours brave Lions. Second place was not invented for these gold-medal fans. Leonians can be competitive to a fault and should remember that there is more to life than winning. At times, they are exhausting to behold, but fortunately there is plenty to love. What they lack in modesty, Leonians make up for in loyalty and are known for being fiercely committed to loved ones and personal goals. At their best, these charismatic leaders rule with a generous heart and visionary mind.

THE LION

It's hard to miss Leonians when they proudly stride into a room. These beings are the kings and queens of their jungle and expect to be treated as such. Give Leonians the royal treatment and they'll be purring sweetly. However, contradict or disrespect them, and get ready to hear their roar. This sign is fierce but loyal. As true leaders of their pack, Leonians can readily be relied on by their loved ones for giving guidance or doing a favour. Strength and courage are usually the Leonian approach, but they also have a side as soft and beautiful as a Lion's mane. The body part associated with Leo is the heart, and these Lions have big ones. Romance from Leonians will be dramatic and bold. Their lovers should expect to be serenaded in the street or proposed to via a message written in the sky. Go big or go home could be the Leonian mantra, because they were not born to blend into the masses.

THE SUN

The Sun sits at the centre of the universe, and those born under the sign of Leo naturally assume the same position. This makes them charismatic and popular, and, just like the Sun, their absence is felt on days when they are not around. Conversely, there are times when Leonians blaze too forcefully, and those around them must seek shade! However, Leonians can heal just as they can hurt. Apollo is known as one of the Greek gods of the Sun, recognised in part for his ability to heal and protect. Apollo was also associated with music and the arts, a contributing factor perhaps to why this Sun-led sign is drawn to taking centre stage. Whether it's pursuing a creative career in the arts or not, the Sun's influence means Leonians usually have a strong sense of who they are and where they are going in life.

ELEMENTS, MODES AND POLARITIES

Each sign is made up of a unique combination of three defining groups: elements, modes and polarities. Each of these defining parts can manifest themselves in good and bad ways and none should be seen as a positive or a negative – including the polarities! Just like a jigsaw puzzle, piecing these groups together can help illuminate why each sign has certain characteristics and help us find a balance.

ELEMENTS

Fire: Dynamic and adventurous, signs with fire in them can be extroverted. Others are naturally drawn to them because of the positive light they give off, as well as their high levels of energy and confidence.

Earth: Signs with the earth element are steady and driven with their ambitions. They make for a solid friend, parent or partner due to their grounded influence and nurturing nature.

Air: The invisible element that influences each of the other elements significantly, air signs will provide much-needed perspective to others with their fair thinking, verbal skills and key ideas.

Water: Warm in the shallows, but sometimes as freezing as ice. This mysterious element is essential to the growth of everything around it, through its emotional depth and empathy.

MODES

Cardinal: Pioneers of the calendar, cardinal signs jump-start each season and are the energetic go-getters.

Fixed: Marking the middle of the calendar, fixed signs firmly denote and value steadiness and reliability.

Mutable: As the seasons end, the mutable signs adapt and give themselves over gladly to the promise of change.

POLARITIES

Positive: Typically extroverted, positive signs take physical action and embrace outside stimulus in their life.

Negative: Usually introverted, negative signs value emotional development and experiencing life from the inside out.

LEO IN BRIEF

The table below shows the key attributes of Leonians. Use it for quick reference and to understand more about this fascinating sign.

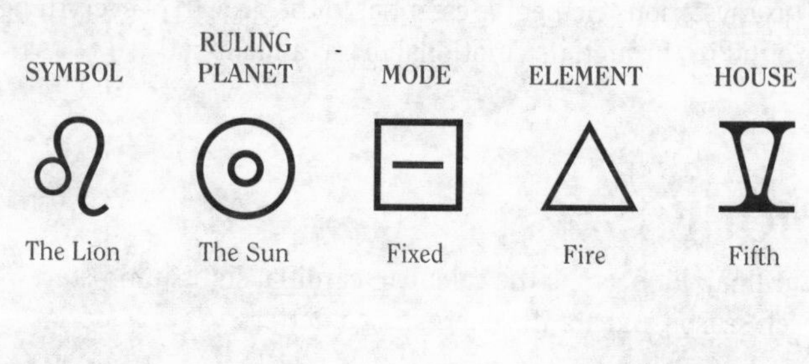

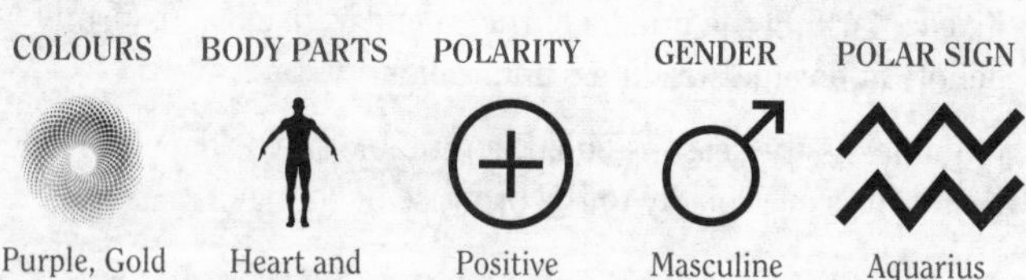

ROMANTIC RELATIONSHIPS

Leonians are associated with the heart, which is perhaps why they appear to love being in love. They take great pleasure in moving heaven and Earth to romance the socks off their love interests. A Bridget Jones-style kiss in the snow or even standing at the front of a ship like Jack and Rose, these brave Lions will romance their partners as well as any romcom movie character. Whether such bold statements of love appeal is a question of personal taste, yet it's difficult not to fall head over heels for these charismatic charmers.

Leonians are the performers of the calendar and have no problem having all admiring eyes on them. Throw roses at their feet and they will likely provide an encore. Clap too enthusiastically, however, and the Leonian ego may take over. They appreciate partners that shower them with praise, but they should try not to demand it. Practising modesty and channelling a quieter confidence can make Leonians even more charming.

Although the demands of Leonians in love can be great, they will give themselves wholeheartedly to their partners. No expense will be spared in their generous gestures of romance, but it will be their staggering displays of loyalty that will probably be appreciated the most. Once they have set their sights on someone, they will be honest and faithful until the end. Leonians have a fearless approach to love, which can mean that they open themselves up to plenty of heartbreak. Yet their courage is contagious, and their willingness to take risks can lead to the biggest rewards in love.

ARIES: COMPATIBILITY 2/5

Arians are used to being first, but they'll have to learn to share the spotlight and decision-making if they fall for a leader of the jungle. These two signs should recognise clearly their similarities, and therefore know just how to advise and support one another in reaching their goals. With the Leonian led by the heart and the Arian by the head, arguments can be a roaring battlefield when these two don't see eye to eye. Ego and pride will need to be kept in check on both sides if this relationship is to go the distance.

TAURUS: COMPATIBILITY 3/5

Leo is ruled by the Sun and Taurus by Venus; this star and planet are never further than 48 degrees from each other. The love that these two share is solidified in their sometimes-stubborn commitment to one another. The Lion and Bull are both fixed signs, and this can be their undoing in a long-term relationship when neither one is willing to compromise. Both the Lion and Bull will shower each other with affection and admiration, and will boost each other's self-esteem and be a positive influence in their careers. This couple should just be careful to not let their egos get in the way.

GEMINI: COMPATIBILITY 4/5

The inner Leonian child can be just what the youthful sign of Gemini asked for. This pairing can be like a children's story full of love and adventure; think Peter Pan and Wendy. The high-energy Leonian was born to lead, whilst the mutable Geminian is happy to take this Lion's hand and fly speedily off to Neverland! The Leonian will encourage the Geminian to take an active part in the important choices in their lives. Both positive signs, their extrovert energies and curious natures will see this air and fire match embarking on endless adventures.

CANCER: COMPATIBILITY 1/5

Leo is ruled by the Sun and Cancer by the Moon, so this pairing can feel as different as night and day. However, the Lion and the Crab can also find that they have plenty in common to form a lasting love. Born in the fourth and fifth houses that partly signify family and children, the Leonian and Cancerian share a fundamental desire to find that long-term partner to settle down with. Security is essential for the Cancerian and the fixed side of the steadfast Leonian can provide just that. This power couple could go the distance if their differences are embraced.

LEO: COMPATIBILITY 3/5

When a Leonian loves a Leonian, it's like stars colliding and causing a supernova explosion. Beautiful and dramatic, these two creatives are naturally pulled together. With so many Leonians using their talents for the dramatics in the arts, this fiery partnership could readily spark on the set of a movie or from working together in some other creative industry. Actors Ben Affleck and Jennifer Lopez are a prime example. However, like with Affleck and Lopez, a long future together is not always guaranteed. Whilst the fun and romance will be plenty, these two fixed signs may struggle to cooperate.

VIRGO: COMPATIBILITY 2/5

The love of a Leonian can take a Virgoan by surprise, which isn't something the introverted Virgoan is always keen on. The clear differences between the studious Virgoan and show-stopping Leonian can mean that these two might be quick to write each other off as potential partners at first glance. The relationship between this fire and earth couple can be a slow burner, but their slow and steady approach could well end up with these two winning the race hand in hand. This couple's strengths are their differences, and these two hard workers can make for a solid and complementary couple.

LIBRA: COMPATIBILITY 4/5

Sitting two places apart on the calendar, a Libran and Leonian can share a compatible partnership. The Libran is an expert in diplomacy, so will likely be able to handle the more dramatic moments in this love affair without bruising the Leonian's ego. Love with the Leonian can be a roller coaster, fun but also consisting of ups and downs. The Libran, symbolised by scales, will hopefully bring a balance to the relationship that the reliable Leonian will appreciate. Ruled by the Sun and Venus, the Leonian and Libran are capable of forming a relationship that is filled with warmth and love.

SCORPIO: COMPATIBILITY 1/5

The love between watery Scorpio and fiery Leo can be one of deep intimacy or dampened spirits. Here are two fixed signs that could clash in their different approaches, as they refuse to yield to each other's strong personalities. Shared assets, particularly money, could prove difficult for them. Scorpio is born in the eighth house where shared possessions are important, and Leo belongs in the fourth house where a love of gambling resides. This could result in serious conflict for the couple. If respect is exercised regularly between these two lovers, theirs is a closeness well worth protecting.

SAGITTARIUS: COMPATIBILITY 4/5

This fire sign match will surely spark with excitement. Here is a couple in which both partners are likely to plan a surprise romantic getaway for the other with little or no notice. Both spontaneous and adventurous, the Leonian and Sagittarian match each other with their positive energies. They are probably the dynamic couple that is at the top of every party invite list. It's not all glittering events, though. The philosophical Sagittarian and purpose-led Leonian can share a powerful bond, with an influence that is felt beyond just them.

CAPRICORN: COMPATIBILITY 4/5

A Leonian and Capricornian are the success love story of when opposites attract. Both tend to have a clear sense of purpose. For the Leonian, it is in their personal life, and for the Capricornian it is in their career. Leonian Barack Obama and Capricornian Michelle Obama are an ideal example of how well these two can work towards achieving their dreams together. The Capricornian can show the Leonian what hard work can accomplish, and the Leonian can bring the fun that sometimes the cool and dignified Capricornian can be lacking. These are two very strong characters that can be even stronger together.

AQUARIUS: COMPATIBILITY 5/5

Aquarius is the air sign that sparks the embers of Leo's fire element into full blaze. Opposites on the calendar, this combination of shared positive energy, fixed attitudes and complementary elements makes for two individuals that were astrologically meant to be. These unique characters can be guilty of feeling superior to others, so may need to remind themselves to treat each other as their rightful equals. Foremost, this is a friendship sprung from fun and crafted by a shared creativity. The visionary mind of the Leonian combined with the Aquarian's ideals could have these two creating a utopic life together.

PISCES: COMPATIBILITY 2/5

When a Leonian meets a Piscean, they can bring out the best and worst in each other. The Piscean can be a source of emotional encouragement for the Leonian, whilst the Leonian could help the dreamy Piscean take more action in their life to fully realise dreams. Born in the twelfth house representing sacrifice, the Piscean can be selfless. The Sun-ruled Leonian can be the opposite. When these two sacrificing and self-serving characteristics are felt at their extremes, the relationship can turn toxic. However, the mutable Piscean and fixed Leonian can live in harmony if they both value each other's best qualities.

FAMILY AND FRIENDS

All great leaders have a loyal following of subjects, and intrepid Leonians are no exception. Like the Sun, they have the power to draw their friends and families outside so that they can spend time in their warm embrace. Being around heartfelt Lions can lift people's spirits and bring huge amounts of fun and joy. Their outgoing and extroverted energy can be contagious, but it can also be tiring. Fellow positive signs could make for great high-energy friends that can easily keep up with these social butterflies. More introverted negative signs can also play an important role. A Leonian will appreciate a friend or family member for whom they don't have to constantly put on a performance. They offer an important change of pace, and an opportunity to recharge.

All the love and support that Leonians receive from their family and friends, they will give back threefold. They are most known for their unparalleled generosity. Leonians love luxury, so their gifts can be extravagant, whether they have the cash to spoil their loved ones or not. If their bank accounts aren't quite big enough to indulge friends, Leonians can be creative even on the most frugal of budgets. Leonians will share money if they have it but, more importantly, they will always give their valued time and energy to relationships.

Belonging to the fifth house in the calendar that is closely associated with children, the protective and high-spirited Leonian can make a wonderful and empathetic parent. In some ways, Leonians never grow up so can remember the frustrations of being young. Their inner children will bring the fun and energy required into raising offspring, or they will

be the fun aunt or uncle that their nieces and nephews always want to play with. If Leonians do not have children of their own, other people's will no doubt still gravitate towards them. This often means Leonians are happy to be the go-to babysitter or first choice of godparent.

Whilst sunny Leonians can have a warm and healing quality, their stage-hogging presence can be overpowering and destructive to their relationships. Their presence and roar is as loud as a Lion's, and it risks drowning out everyone else. It may not be the intention of Leonians to overshadow their friends and family, but the self-led influence from their guiding Sun can turn this confident ruler into a bossy dictator. Their fixed attitudes can make them resistant to the different opinions of others, but Leonians should be careful of surrounding themselves with only yes-men. A diverse social network where everyone has a voice is the only kingdom worthy of Leonian leadership.

MONEY AND CAREERS

Being a particular star sign will not dictate that you follow a certain type of career, but it can help you to identify potential areas for thriving in. Conversely, to succeed in the workplace, it is just as important to understand strengths and weaknesses to achieve career and financial goals.

A love for luxury and aristocratic tendencies creates a risk for Leonians to become too focused on the material things in life. It can be good to enjoy a little luxury in life, as long as they don't let it dominate everything they do. However, if they can channel their love for grand things creatively, they could follow in the footsteps of notable Leonian fashion designers such as Yves Saint-Laurent, Coco Chanel and Michael Kors. Rather than wearing the designer names of others, Leonians possess a passion for luxury and leadership that could help them become the next big name that everyone is coveting.

Whilst Leonians enjoy the best in life, they will generally be sensible with their finances and not spend beyond their means. A trip to Vegas might be tempting, but they aren't usually the type to go for broke and risk losing it all. The fixed part of Leonians will keep their spending steady, unwilling to risk losing their financial security. They may be driven to earn lots of money so that they can buy all the luxuries they desire, but they will probably earn their fortune through organised efforts and a steadfast approach rather than at the slot machines.

Whether Leonians go for the leading roles in a film or strive after leading a country, they will be comfortable in the spotlight of their choice. Leonians' natural self-assurance makes them authoritative and confident figures, and others

will respect that, if given the opportunity. So whether it's the moves of Leonian Mick Jagger, the skills of Harry Kane or the leadership of Barack Obama, all eyes will be firmly on them.

If fame doesn't appeal, managerial roles could be a natural domain in many industries, be it on a football field or in an office. Occupations in the world of luxury are also appealing, given Leonians' appreciation of the finer things in life. But no matter the field, being boss is often the primary goal, although a bossy attitude should to be avoided wherever possible to keep others happy.

As with family, colleagues cannot be chosen. Therefore, it can be advantageous to use star signs to learn about their key characteristics and discover the best ways of working together. Part of the attraction for becoming a leader for Leonians is the competition. The king or queen of the jungle loves to demonstrate their prowess and rise above any competitors. However, Leonians can be dominating and may need to remind themselves that there is no 'I' in 'team', especially if they are working with other 'me first' characters, such as Arians. Taureans might share the same ambitious dreams as Leonians, but any colleague that is also fixed will need to work harder at finding a place to compromise.

HEALTH AND WELLBEING

These bold Lions can also be highly sensitive souls. Like anyone, they have their ups and downs, so friends and family can be essential supporters that straighten the crown on their ruler's head. The critical words of Virgoans might be felt too harshly by sensitive Leonians, and knock their confidence further if they are already feeling low. Pisceans or Cancerians could tread more carefully, and be the emotionally encouraging friends that help Leonians stride forwards again. A need for constant reassurance can stem from a crisis in confidence, so Leonians should work on building up their own self-esteem from within so that they do not have to always rely on others to lift them out of their low moods. Owning their mistakes and recognising where they can improve are just a couple of ways that Leonians can grow to become happier and humble.

Winning can feel wonderful, but when Leonians reach their desired peak, they may find themselves at a loss. Once Leonians rise to the top of their profession, they may need to take up another hobby or avenue of interest to satisfy their urge to win. Throwing themselves into a competitive sport that takes them outside will appease their ambitious side, youthful energy and love of the Sun. Whilst protection from harmful UV rays is important, spending time in the Sun sensibly can be just as vital for keeping healthy. Apart from receiving essential Vitamin D, sunshine's healing properties also extend to lowering cholesterol and reducing high blood pressure – wonderful news for heart-associated Leonians. Learning lines for their latest play in the sunshine, or swimming in a lido rather than an indoor swimming pool, could also help improve physical and mental health.

HEALTH AND WELLBEING

Guided by the Sun, representing the self and life purpose, Leonians seem to know who they are and where they are going. At least that's what it can look like from the standpoint of admiring onlookers. If Leonians lack direction in life, it can be a major source of upset for them. They may feel they are not living up to their own expectations or the expectations of others. Leonians should try to take the pressure off themselves, and understand that learning who they truly are and where they wish to get to in life are two big questions that plague everyone. They would do well to cut themselves some slack, and not get bogged down by their reputation of always being the best. The high status of the charismatic, larger-than-life Lion can be a burden to Leonians that feel they don't fit the bill. They are essentially best at being themselves, whatever form that may take, so should not attempt to cage themselves within the confines of expectation.

Leo

DAILY FORECASTS for 2021

OCTOBER

Friday 1st

You're more empowered today as the Moon is back in your sign. An urge to push through boundaries and restrictions is irresistible and commendable if you need to be productive. However, leave personal boundaries untouched for now. Expect delays with communications and chores today as Mercury makes unhelpful connections.

Saturday 2nd

Be very careful in your dealings with people higher than you today. The Moon is opposing Jupiter who stands for law and order but also connects to Uranus the disruptor. Your leadership qualities may be challenged. If you're a weekend worker, be mindful of upsetting the boss.

Sunday 3rd

It's possible to make amends with someone today. Mercury is connecting to Jupiter. Remember that retrogrades are not meant to trip you up but are chances for you to 'do over'. Review, revisit and rethink a recent confrontation and put things right today.

Monday 4th

Money is on your mind now. Check any financial arrangements you have with another person as there may be a payment overdue. This is a good time to make sure your home affairs are in order even if it's just clearing a messy spot. You may discover something you thought lost.

Tuesday 5th

You make changes that affect your duties and obligations to others. This will free up some time for you to concentrate on your own interests. Well done, you're practising self-care by making time for yourself. These small steps will gain momentum until you're completely in charge of your schedule.

Wednesday 6th

Planetary energy is high today. There is a new moon in your communication sector right next to Mars. Think of this as a supercharged time to make goals and intentions that will likely stick. Pluto turns direct and self-control will become easier. Mars and Pluto are formidable allies.

Thursday 7th

Venus is about to leave your family sector. Is there anything outstanding that needs attention here before she moves? Honour your female relatives and take note of any women's wisdom passed down to you today. A deeply nurturing and secretive Moon will take her place for the next two days.

Friday 8th

The Sun and Mars meet today and activity ramps up. Your communication sector will be busier than ever, but you have the energy from Mars to deal with it. There may be high productivity or massive ego clashes. Make sure that there are no misunderstandings and enjoy this energetic time.

Saturday 9th

This is a difficult day emotionally. First, you're tempted to switch off and do nothing, then you're reluctantly coaxed outside to join in some fun. Your creative and passionate side just wants to play today. Romance is favoured but be careful that playfulness doesn't turn nasty.

Sunday 10th

Saturn turns direct in your relationship sector today. This will ease some of the pressure and allow you to begin making moves to get to know someone better. The Moon connects nicely to other planets making this a day where you are more emotionally balanced. Have a peaceful day.

Monday 11th

Your energy is buoyant today and you start the working week with a smile. Projects that bring out your artistic side are easily tackled. People will admire the way you take on tasks and make them a priority. This is a happy day; make the most of the energy.

Tuesday 12th

Expect to be pleasantly surprised at work. This could be that you discover something or solve a problem. You will be recognised as a dependable member of the team today as you work through the day steadily. Take small steps to begin a task that has so far looked insurmountable.

Wednesday 13th

The Moon meets newly direct Pluto today. Issues of power and control come under discussion. Where might you have let someone else lead the way? Do you now need to take charge? They meet in your health and duties sector so this could also concern your personal wellbeing.

Thursday 14th

In your relationship sector, the Moon now meets Saturn, also newly direct. Partnerships will benefit from a frank discussion today. Over the summer months, relationships may have been strained but will begin to settle into a pattern that is mutually beneficial. This may feel unusual but will work.

Friday 15th

The Sun and Jupiter combine to bring you some good luck and advice today. Listen to any words coming from fathers, male elders or bosses as this will stand you in good stead in the long run. This stern paternal energy is also filled with joy and optimism.

Saturday 16th

The Moon enters your intimacy sector today. You contemplate where you're going from here. Do you wish to get to know someone or something on a deeper level or are you afraid to? The mysteries of life such as sex, death and rebirth both fascinate and repel you.

Sunday 17th

Jupiter turns direct today. You may experience this as a huge sigh of relief. If you've been confused about relationship issues weighing on you, you may now see a way forward. The Moon sits with Neptune making your emotions a little foggy but this will pass soon. Listen to your inner voice.

Monday 18th

The trickster Mercury turns direct now. While he has been in your communications sector, you may have had to slow down or pause your mental faculties. You have found this frustrating. Now you can think, plan and communicate without misunderstanding once more. An action-packed Moon will help.

Tuesday 19th

You're emotionally invested in doing something more valuable with your spare time. Long distance travel or higher education call you. The Moon sits opposite Mercury and you must now evaluate the long-term investments of study and travel. Perhaps you can combine these with a work vacation?

Wednesday 20th

There's a full moon in your travel sector today. This is the culmination of the last six months of planning and discovering. Has it been worthwhile? You may feel emotionally drained and despondent today. Maybe not all your goals have come to fruition. Don't beat yourself up about it.

Thursday 21st

You are feeling down, and tears may be very near the surface. Your work environment is not satisfying you today. The Moon sits with Uranus making you unstable, but you can also use this energy to come up with something new and innovative. Get up and make a difference.

Friday 22nd

Let yourself dream a little now. Replace negative thinking with something to cheer you up. Splash out on a fine dining experience and don't feel guilty about it. Use your hard-earned cash on something to make you smile.

Saturday 23rd

The Sun enters your family sector and will warm up interactions here. In this deeply intense sign, you may find that people bond more or reveal their secret worries. Your social sector is visited by the Moon and you're desperate to connect with your wider groups and let off some steam.

Sunday 24th

Mercury and Venus are connecting to the Moon today. Your social life is full of plans and conversation. A lover may wish to do something different to the group and this could cause you some conflict. You will need Mercury's skills as a mediator to work around this problem.

Monday 25th

Your mind is very busy today. Active Mars is busy trying to keep everyone happy whilst optimistic Jupiter is attempting to appease problems with your relationship. Neptune tries to drag you away for some peace, but you are determined to make peace with others before getting time for yourself.

Tuesday 26th

Venus and Neptune are squaring off today. You may be acting out and having mini-tantrums with a lover. The Moon is in your hidden sector and you simply need to be left alone to take care of yourself. This may be more like licking your wounds; growl safely in your own home.

Wednesday 27th

When you are in self-protect mode, there is always someone who wants to pull you out of it. Practise what you've learned this year and come out when you're ready. Communications are too emotionally charged today, say nothing or risk a new cause to fight.

Thursday 28th

The Moon reaches your sign by late morning. Until then you may be extra sensitive and defensive. There's a risk that you show off and become obnoxious as your mood has not abated yet. Rules and regulations annoy you and you may find your inner rebel rises up. Sit tight, this will ease.

Friday 29th

Conflict in the workplace keeps you on your toes. You may find yourself arguing your case in order to keep the peace. Mercury is still in your communications sector and you can draw on his energy to help you speak honestly and clearly. Don't get drawn into unnecessary dramas.

Saturday 30th

Ego clashes are possible as the Sun and Saturn are at odds. Family members and important relationships need your attention. Mars has just marched into your family sector so expect the bigger pull to come from there. You feel stuck between a rock and a hard place.

Sunday 31st

You feel the need to bring order out of chaos. Built-up tension from recent days needs an outlet. DIY projects or a deep clean of your home will be worthwhile activities today. You know you always feel better by making a change or having a clear out of unwanted items.

NOVEMBER

Monday 1st

Use your powers of persuasion to ask for what you want today. Mercury is making a helpful connection to Jupiter in your relationships sector. Think of a dream or vision you wish to share with someone special and vocalise it. You may just want to make a few small changes.

Tuesday 2nd

The Moon now dips into your communications sector and you are emotionally invested in sharing information that will help bring balance. What are you passionate about that needs to be heard by others? Stay in control but refrain from being pushy; elders are listening.

Wednesday 3rd

Mercury now greets the Moon. You may find that your heart and head are in sync and whatever comes out of your mouth does so with utmost conviction. You want fairness and equality now. It seems like it's up to you to address any imbalance that has transpired recently.

Thursday 4th

Today can be highly volatile or powerful. The New Moon in your family sector is asking for a big change, starting from now. Connections to Uranus and Mars mean that things could get disruptive. Use this powerful energy to brainstorm the best solution for all involved. No secrets, no lies.

Friday 5th

The Sun sits opposite Uranus and challenges the disruptive planet. You may witness a stand-off where someone has to account for their rebellious actions. Mercury is going to eke out family ghosts whilst Venus prefers that you simply do your daily duties and not get involved. This is a testing time.

Saturday 6th

Today you may feel creative or poetic. Your inner child wishes to come out to play. Take a break from adulting and enjoy some childlike fun. Venus reminds Mercury that if he must go opening old wounds, to do it with kindness and with a view to getting them healed.

Sunday 7th

Joyous Jupiter tunes into your need for play today. As the luck-bringer, he can see that you need to feel free, even if just for a little while. Don't let Neptune seduce you into switching off with things such as alcohol. Keep it safe and enjoy some laughter today.

Monday 8th

The Moon and Venus have a ladies' night. Many planets connect to allow you to tap into feminine wisdom or enjoy the company of women. You have a list of small chores but can work through them steadily and be pleased with your results by the end of the day.

Tuesday 9th

You may now get an idea of what the new moon brought up. What needs to change? Pluto is asking that you end something and clear the decks to make way for something new. If you're afraid of change and resist it, then Pluto will do it for you.

Wednesday 10th

This is a tricky day with tough planetary energy. You desire to reach out and feel the love with a partner but Mercury and Mars have met up. This energy can be very argumentative or sexually persuasive. Saturn is also involved, so be very mindful of pushing people's boundaries.

Thursday 11th

The air is still sizzling with tension in your relationships. Uranus is waiting to blow it all up in your face. Jupiter jumps on board and can either make outbursts larger or disperse it all with his joyful nature. How you play it is up to you.

Friday 12th

The Sun in your intense family sector is burning away illusions set up by Neptune. It's likely that you will now see a situation for what it really is. Those ghosts in the family closet may be ready to be exposed. You feel stunned and do not know how to act.

Saturday 13th

Compassion and empathy are your two best allies today. There is still unsavoury stuff emerging from your family sector. You are asked to look at things from another's point of view. Mercury opposite Uranus does not help. This is unstable energy so expect rows and plenty of tears.

Sunday 14th

You're not comfortable with this emotional energy and need to be in your own element. This afternoon the Moon moves into your travel sector and offers you a distraction. Make plans for yourself; be selfish if it means disassociating with other people's dramas. Let your brain do the talking.

Monday 15th

Be aware that those close to you are watching how you handle conflict. You must be the leader that your fiery sign represents. It may be hard for you to get on with your daily routine, but you must do so for your own sanity. Stick to your agenda today.

Tuesday 16th

Resistance will come from your duties sector and interfere with the plans you are making in your head. You must double-check that you can commit to new ideas to travel or study. Perhaps this is not achievable, and you already have too much going on.

Wednesday 17th

The focus is on your career today and there too, you find blocks preventing you from realising your dreams. Mars is now opposite Uranus meaning that your roles at work and at home are under fire. Be sure of your responsibilities before taking off on your own path.

Thursday 18th

You are ready to blow today. Don't let temporary setbacks cause you to lose face and show your lion's roar. You may say something that you don't mean or shouldn't voice out loud. If you use this energy wisely, you may finally get to the bottom of something deep.

Friday 19th

A full moon in your career sector will put you in the spotlight. You are being observed so you must be on top form. Tie up loose ends and complete projects before the weekend arrives. Lighten your load and let those who are watching see how capable you are.

Saturday 20th

The Moon is in your social sector just in time for you to have some downtime with friends. If you stay home alone, your mind will be doing overtime and you won't switch off. Mercury and Jupiter connect, making family interactions great fun or highly controversial, probably the latter.

Sunday 21st

During your interactions with your wider social groups, you may find that not all your dreams are possible. You might feel disappointed and need time to process this. Neptune is coaxing you to follow a path that is just an illusion. Get more grounded and get advice from friends.

Monday 22nd

You return to self-protect mode today as the Moon enters your hidden sector. Factor in some time to shop for your favourite foods and schedule a good book or film. The Sun has shifted into your creative sector. You may feel extra sensitive and need to express your deepest feelings.

Tuesday 23rd

Today you reflect on the years gone by and what you have left behind. This does not come without some sorrow. Venus wants you to get on with your daily routine and get some stability but you are wallowing in the past. Remember the good lessons you can use now.

Wednesday 24th

That familiar nagging takes you away from your comfort zone before you are ready. The Moon dips into your sign and you become resentful and sulky. Mercury leaves your family sector having dug up some dirt and leaving a big hole. Deal with it and heal it.

Thursday 25th

If you are open to it, today can be romantic and passionate. The fiery Moon in your sign opposes Saturn but you wish to connect with someone special. Venus and Mars make this possible by finding time to play nicely. Your ruler, the Sun, is in your romantic sector so take advantage.

Friday 26th

Be mindful of how you're putting yourself across today. You are bold and brash but may come across as selfish and narcissistic. Wanting your own way is one thing but do not do it at the expense of someone important to you. They will remind you of this.

Saturday 27th

Over the weekend, make yourself feel better by organising your home and finances. You're not in the mood for social interactions so use this time to declutter and check your bank balance. Decluttering your environment helps to declutter your mind. This will leave you feeling fresh and receptive.

Sunday 28th

Neptune nags at you to relax and kick back. Ignoring this call and continuing to do personal admin will serve you better. By the end of the day, you will be so pleased with yourself that you make an impulse buy and treat yourself. A simple takeaway meal will suffice.

Monday 29th

Mercury is in the heat of the Sun today. He talks to your ruler and you have a good think about your recent behaviour. Today's a day for listening and not speaking. Being quiet but taking in messages from within you will provide you with plenty of food for thought.

Tuesday 30th

Your emotions are more balanced today. There is some resistance about doing your daily chores or helping someone, but you don't take this too seriously. You have a duty of care to others and you willingly oblige. You have time to relax and be alone later today.

DECEMBER

Wednesday 1st

Neptune moves direct today. A new Neptune cycle asks you to turn within and listen to your inner voice. Anything you have been struggling with in your intimacy sector will now become clearer. The deeper mysteries of life and your desire for something bigger will now be more tangible.

Thursday 2nd

Whilst in your family sector, the Moon connects to Neptune and you may see things with different eyes. This can be a revelation or an upset, but will soon be smoothed over and peace will be restored. You may hear "I told you so" from an elder or a life teacher.

Friday 3rd

A meeting with Mars can make your emotions more volatile today. It can also provide fuel for brave, new action you need to take. You must be firm in your dealings with family. This afternoon it is easier to speak your truth with compassion and maybe even laughter.

Saturday 4th

Today there's a new moon in your creative sector. An outgoing mood will help you set intentions to be who you truly are. Maybe you have an idea about what your sacred purpose is now. Listen to Mercury's messages as when he meets the Moon he may have some good advice.

Sunday 5th

A Sunday afternoon spent with a loved one can be pleasant. You find that you're more willing to share your innermost feelings. Discussions about where you would like to travel to or what you desire to learn can be filled with joy and optimism. Your partner shares your vision.

Monday 6th

One step at a time is the best way to achieve your goals today. Tasks at work or in your daily life are near to completion. Mars and Pluto connect to give you the strength and energy to finish a long-standing project before the festive season begins.

Tuesday 7th

You may be emotionally invested in something that you now need to let go of. Remember that when there is space, new things can take shape. Pluto helps you to lovingly remove what has reached its expiry date. You will have more time for love and connection with special people.

Wednesday 8th

Today may be a little edgy when the Moon meets Saturn. Think of a harsh teacher with a very important lesson for you. You may not want to hear it but it's truly beneficial that you do. Family, career and partnerships are all involved in this. Be humble and listen.

Thursday 9th

Worries and concerns may feel bigger than they actually are. A boss or leader might touch a sensitive spot in you today. Take some time to pause and reflect on how you were triggered. Self-talk doesn't need to be negative; praise yourself for the good you have done.

Friday 10th

A more peaceful day today where you spend time contemplating the last year. Revelations come but are gentle and make you smile. There may be a nice surprise coming from your career sector or a breakthrough of ongoing problems. Try not to fill up your day with tasks.

Saturday 11th

Your mood continues to be dreamy and contemplative. Spending time alone with your thoughts helps you to justify a few things. Venus and Pluto meet up in your health and duties sector. This is a day to put yourself first and pay attention to your body. Listen to what it needs.

Sunday 12th

As the Moon shifts into your travel sector, you are more active and begin making lists. A vision board of places of interest can be a fun activity. The Venus and Pluto connection asks that you make changes with solid steps to reach your goals. Don't let anyone sway you.

Monday 13th

Two planets change sign today. Mercury now enters your health and duties sector helping you research any missing information you need. Mars marches into your creative sector and can either bring you the energy to stand up for yourself or can make you amorous and look for love.

Tuesday 14th

A small setback halts your plans today. You have a moment of conscience and wonder whether you are being too selfish. Your sense of security depends on your career income and you don't wish to jeopardise this. Wait until you have all the facts that Mercury will bring.

Wednesday 15th

Tension is building inside you. This is your old way of thinking and you must remember that it no longer serves your best interests. Take time to breathe and get grounded today. Take a walk in nature, do yoga or spoil yourself with an impulse buy.

Thursday 16th

You put your worries to one side as there is too much going on now that the festive season approaches. Self-control helps you to work through your task list with ease and time spare to dream. If dreaming about a possible future makes you happy, keep doing it.

Friday 17th

The Moon dips into your social sector just in time for some weekend fun. You're in demand now and there will be a lot to chat about with friends you may not have seen for a long time. An opposition to Mars can mean that your social interactions will drain your energy.

Saturday 18th

Venus turns retrograde tonight. She will do this in your health and duties sector. You may find that you forget how to look after yourself now and burn the midnight oil. Expect a lover from the past to suddenly make a reappearance. Squabbles with a lover are possible now.

Sunday 19th

A full moon in your social sector will highlight the culmination of a project with friends. Maybe a course of study has come to an end. This can be a lively time with your online interactions and wider groups. By this evening you want your own space.

Monday 20th

The Moon in your hidden sector connects to Mercury and Uranus today. It's possible that something you would prefer to be kept secret is revealed and upsets you. Alternatively, you may wish to disclose something about yourself and this courageous action surprises you. Stay safe and keep your boundaries strong today.

Tuesday 21st

The winter solstice is here. The longest night is a time to lie low and contemplate. Treat yourself to home comforts as much as you can today and celebrate the longer days to come. Do whatever it takes to feel protected even if that means avoiding certain company.

Wednesday 22nd

Your sign is visited by the Moon for the final time this year. You feel more outgoing and join in the celebrations of the season. You can shine like a true leader today. Be warned, your tendency to go over the top can make you obnoxious. Lead with compassion and a true heart.

Thursday 23rd

Jupiter is at the final degree of your relationship sector for the second time this year. It's critical that you answer his call to sort something out once and for all. Remember that Jupiter stands for truth, justice and expansion. If you wish to know someone better, tell them.

Friday 24th

Tension is building as you would expect at this time of year. The areas affected for you are your home and finances. Do not be forced to host the celebrations if you cannot afford to. Be firm with people and tell them exactly how much you are prepared to do.

Saturday 25th

Venus returns to meet Pluto today. This is synonymous with control issues concerning women. Is there someone who is doing more than their fair share? Is this you? Ask for help or step in and give assistance to another. Make the day go without unnecessary hitches.

Sunday 26th

You just cannot rest today. You are like a prowling lion in a cage. If you're in your own home, you clear up any mess caused by the celebrations. You don't like to let it linger. This afternoon brings you back to a balanced frame of mind.

Monday 27th

The Moon in your communications sector helps you to deal with short trips and messages. Maybe the social side of the celebrations isn't over and you still have people to see. You have the energy to do your duty by your family and you behave like a responsible adult. Well done.

Tuesday 28th

The energy is much more difficult today. You do your best to make sure that all around you are happy but you cannot please everyone. Power struggles come from your health and duties sector and spoil the day. Let others sort out their own problems for now.

Wednesday 29th

The Moon is in your family sector and your mood may be intense. Saturn and Uranus are involved so expect to be involved in a disturbance. Jupiter bounces into your intimacy sector where he'll make you inquisitive about life's deeper mysteries. Get ready to explore and discover the depth and breadth of everything.

Thursday 30th

It's possible that you can use persuasive words to control a situation that has become out of hand. Mercury is with Pluto and between them, they investigate what may have gone wrong. You will be completely drained by evening. Get some rest.

Friday 31st

Mars gives you the energy you need to party through the night. You can let off steam and thoroughly enjoy the evening. As the Moon has met Mars today, a New Year romance could be out there waiting for you. Have a great New Year's Eve.

Leo

DAILY FORECASTS for 2022

JANUARY

....

Saturday 1st

Happy New Year and welcome to 2022. Your year begins with a lack of energy. Perhaps you've partied too hard and need to slow down. There may still be some surprises coming your way, but they could be wrapped in paper that belies the truth of what is underneath. Proceed with caution and try to be realistic about things today.

Sunday 2nd

A new moon gives you a chance to set goals and intentions regarding your mundane duties and career. It could be time to look at the balance here and let go of a few things that are oppressive or unnecessary baggage. Discussions with a lover or business partner may reach a new level.

Monday 3rd

An emotional situation from the past may return to bother you. This is likely to be a one-sided relationship that you may have left a long time ago. Exercise restraint and don't let yourself be pulled back into an unhealthy connection. Give someone the closure they need.

Tuesday 4th

You may cling on to a partner and ask a lot of questions. Be prepared to be answered with the truth, which may not be what you want to hear. Total respect for another person is needed now to avoid any upset. Make sure that you aren't pushing someone's boundaries.

Wednesday 5th

Your drive and passion to be romantic and creative may help you relate to someone special on their level. Self-expression may be quite forceful, and you may need to tread carefully. Alternatively, you could be experiencing a lack of progress and wish to know the underlying reasons why.

Thursday 6th

Delving deeper into the unknown could get you into trouble today. Your emotions may be bigger than usual, but this could present a challenge that erupts in your face. Unrealistic expectations may be the cause now. It could also be that you're too stubborn to accept a viewpoint that differs from yours.

Friday 7th

Trouble could arise with a ghost from the past nudging their way back into your life. This may make you feel like you want to be a little too aggressive and uncompromising. Take a good look at what you want from your life now and make a plan to align yourself with your true north.

Saturday 8th

An outgoing mood may be difficult to appease today. There may be many things that you wish to implement this year including travel opportunities or higher education. Talking about these might lead to lively interaction with a partner. Get out an atlas and stick a pin in it. Set a target for this year.

Sunday 9th

You may still be bothered by a past love or a passion you once held close to your heart. This could play on your mind today. You must resist the urge to pick up where you left off and continue an unhealthy habit or relationship. Put your energy into something new.

Monday 10th

Today you may be fired up to accept a new challenge in the workplace. This could be highly beneficial for you but will need constant reviewing and may not happen at once. Get to the bottom of anything that you find radical or unusual about it. Do your research.

Tuesday 11th

This may be a tricky day as you could be trying to grasp new concepts. Don't worry if this takes a little longer than you'd like. You may feel out of your depth and resort to trying to get your own way. This won't resolve anything and could make matters worse.

Wednesday 12th

Bring your energy down to earth today and do practical activities that you know you can do well. This might boost your confidence and make you feel successful. Something might click into place that helps you to make necessary changes or deal with difficult people.

Thursday 13th

Social groups can be supportive today if you listen to advice from experienced people. Mercury turns retrograde tomorrow, so make some preparations such as double-checking travel plans and backing up all devices. Aim for clear and precise communications in your relationships as this is the area that Mercury will disturb.

Friday 14th

Mercury retrograde begins. You may feel hesitant to make any long-lasting commitment and you would be wise to go with your gut on this. At least wait until retrograde is over. Use this time to review what is offered and consider if it aligns with your personal truths and core values.

Saturday 15th

You might feel drained and emotional today. It would be useful if you can find time for self-care and nurture. You could feel defensive and need familiar things around you now. Turn inwards and give your body, mind and soul a little bit of love. Put your own needs first if you can.

Sunday 16th

Today may be difficult as outside forces could intrude on your alone time. An issue you've ignored is likely asking for attention. Be extremely careful now as you could be prone to rash actions that you will regret later. If you can, it may be best to play it safe and stay home alone.

Monday 17th

A full moon might highlight your weaknesses and trigger you into an emotional time today. You may have a feeling of disconnect in the daytime that is hard to shake off. This could leave you feeling vulnerable to a disagreement that you won't see coming. Stay alert and in control.

Tuesday 18th

The Moon drops into your sign and can raise your fighting spirit. As Uranus turns direct you may have an urge to act out of character or think outside the box. This could also mark a time at work where something new and innovative is beginning for you.

Wednesday 19th

Time to think and process new duties would be better than trying to run before you can walk. You may resist an elder's advice and this could bring out your shadow side. A tantrum is possible; try not to project onto those with whom you work.

Thursday 20th

Get ready for some high activity and insight into your relationships. You might find that you're drawn more to doing something for the greater good. Perhaps you would like to volunteer for a worthy cause. You may find a new passionate pastime now. Check all the details and see if it adds up.

Friday 21st

Your mind and attitude can be more rational today. If a problem needs solving, you could find a practical workaround that is suitable. You may also be dealing with a difficult connection by breaking things down into bite-size pieces. Someone might need to be fed smaller chunks of information.

Saturday 22nd

There is no time for dreaming today as you could be continuing to find loopholes or connecting the dots. This may be playing out financially or in your home environment. You may decide that decluttering your life has to start from what you see around you every day.

Sunday 23rd

Stop and listen for subliminal messages or dream symbols. You may also hear something to your advantage. However, you must not act on it just yet. Store it away until the time is right to use what you learn today. Your mind may go into overdrive if you attempt to process it now.

Monday 24th

Your health may become an issue now. This could be a good time to look at healthy eating or to start a new exercise regime. If you can keep this up for a few weeks, it's more likely to stick and become part of your everyday routine.

Tuesday 25th

Today may bring some challenges, which can provoke intense feelings such as jealousy and manipulation. You might have bitten off more than you can chew and got yourself into a pickle. Try not to jump out of it again too soon as you may end up in a worse predicament.

Wednesday 26th

If you find that you are back-tracking or retreating from challenging circumstances, go easy on yourself. It may simply be that an old routine needs to be relearned. You might need to upgrade your knowledge in a certain area in order to keep up with the times. This can be annoying but beneficial.

Thursday 27th

You might find that moving away from old ways and embracing new ones is not as daunting as you first thought. You may even find it exciting. Look at what advantages this can bring. It could open your world a little wider and bring in more opportunities for growth.

Friday 28th

An outward-looking viewpoint can win you rewards today. An emotional attachment to a duty or service for others will bring you praise and recognition. Get all the information you need to make a good choice now and try not to be deluded or unrealistic about results.

Saturday 29th

Venus turns direct now, and you might notice that you're getting somewhere with a ghost from the past. It may surprise you to learn how much this has affected your performance recently. Let it go with love. Listen carefully to your inner voice as you may get a new personal mission today.

Sunday 30th

It's possible that you have uncomfortable feelings about something you've released. This is perfectly normal, so allow yourself to grieve your loss. A relationship challenge may be disturbing this evening. Do something for yourself that helps you to switch off and relax. Find your inner compass and realign.

Monday 31st

Today you could have more idea of what is expected of you this year. However, remember that Mercury is retrograde, and you shouldn't commit to anything just yet. Look at how the land lies and prepare your ground. If this is meant for you, then you may see an undeniable signpost.

FEBRUARY

....

Tuesday 1st

Old patterns may pop in and out of your head stirring up some deep-seated emotions from your shadow. If you grasp what these are, you may set an intention under the new moon to take back control and work on these issues. Learn to recognise when you project your baggage onto other people.

Wednesday 2nd

You may feel out of your depth as you manage challenging emotions. The answer may be to go as deep as you dare and take a look around. Get motivated to do something that benefits your emotional and physical health. Meditation or another such practice would be good for you.

Thursday 3rd

Try to stay calm today as you might find that you are more sensitive and emotional. This bubbling under the surface may serve to give you some indicators on what needs shifting. Look at your friendship groups to see if there is anything sneaky going on and protect yourself.

Friday 4th

Mercury turns direct today and you could begin to review anything you've postponed recently. Grab hold of your inner compass and align yourself with your core values. Making a grand gesture could be a bold move, but you will need to be able to back it up with direct action.

Saturday 5th

Work duties might clash with your own needs today. You may be frustrated if you have a weekend working and can't get to the gym or to the shops. Unfortunately, you might need to attend to deadlines and may have little time for pleasure. The rewards will come to you later.

Sunday 6th

You may consider this weekend has been wasted and you haven't had enough time for yourself. Negative thinking isn't going to make it any better. Turn this around and look at how productive you've been in other areas of life and give yourself some credit for this. Treat yourself before bedtime.

Monday 7th

The week begins with grounding energy and you could call on your work colleagues for favours. Perhaps you've made yourself available for them in recent times and now you would like something in return. This exchange of energy and service can work well for you as respect is earned.

Tuesday 8th

Watch your temper today as you may come to blows with a person in authority. This may be an example of how you project shadow material onto others when you're stressed or against a wall. Make a note of it and consider the triggers that made you react.

Wednesday 9th

You could be in the mood to connect with your social groups and sound off in a safe place. Here may be the ideal place to process some of your recent behaviours and receive wisdom and advice. Listen carefully to anything that is offered today and be open to learning.

Thursday 10th

Waves of emotions can make you expand and contract depending on who you're dealing with today. Some people will sap your energy, whilst others will add to it and buoy you along with good cheer and motivation. Acknowledge that those who bring you down may not be your tribe.

Friday 11th

If you feel out of sorts today, simply do what is necessary to get by. You may already be winding down and collapsing for the weekend. Listen carefully to the grapevine and your own inner voice as you could hear a new call to adventure. This will feel very attractive today.

Saturday 12th

The celestial lovers, Mars and Venus, are getting ready to meet. This period may mark a time where your masculine and feminine sides merge. You may be thinking and feeling, driven and compassionate about your duties. It might also be a sign that you are taking better care of your own needs.

Sunday 13th

Use today to rest and curl up in your safety zone. A day of nurturing yourself with things you love to do will feed your soul and recharge your batteries. You may feel extra sensitive and nostalgic and could drift away to a fantasy land for the remainder of the day.

Monday 14th

If you feel that you're being dragged from your safety net, remember that you have duties to perform that won't get done without you. You could feel resentful and get stroppy. Conversations with someone special may reach a new level of enquiry now. You may wish to know some unusual facts.

Tuesday 15th

Conflict with authority figures can be troublesome and trigger your darker side again. Watch what you say and do as self-righteous behaviour won't be appreciated. Draw your attention to your health and ability to be available for people unconditionally. Compassionate acts are favoured, which could start something new for you.

Wednesday 16th

A full moon in your sign indicates where you're in the spotlight and can shine your worth into the world. However, you could take this another way and thrust your presence where it isn't wanted. Mars and Venus meet and show you how to take care of your own needs first.

Thursday 17th

Take stock of what you own and what brings you pleasure today. A new and innovative idea appeals to you and you could possibly stumble against a money-making scheme. Attend to something urgent in your relationships or be impulsive and suggest an unusual activity for you both to enjoy.

Friday 18th

Practical activities that require your full attention might occupy you this morning. Your ego may desire to dream and drift away, but you have a good sense of duty and this will bring you back and make sure that all your important chores are done. Be methodical and meticulous with paperwork.

Saturday 19th

Easy-going conversations can bring emotional satisfaction. It might be that you are getting to know someone on a deeper level and finding out what makes them tick. You may be drawn to good causes and wish to help out in your community more. Don't try starting a revolution on your own.

Sunday 20th

You could have a strong sense of your own limits today and this might keep you from doing anything you feel goes against your nature or your principles. Aim for equality and fairness, but always remember to be fair to yourself and attend to your own needs, as well as those of the people around you.

Monday 21st

Intense energy amps up your emotions and you could feel stubborn or unmoving about taking on anything new or arduous. Take some time to think about how this may or may not fit into your schedule. It might just need a few tweaks. Don't take on any more than you can manage.

Tuesday 22nd

A strong sense of justice may cause you to open a can of worms and stir up trouble. This is likely to occur in the workplace. Saying no to something may be the thing that lets you see that you can have strong personal boundaries when necessary.

Wednesday 23rd

A change or release of old habits could be a positive move today. You might wake deciding to transform something you feel strongly about. This can make you more optimistic and outgoing. Romance and creativity are also highlighted, and you may be making changes here that can bring you more joy.

Thursday 24th

Your curious mind knows no bounds today, but you must be careful not to overstep boundaries and get too pushy. You may not notice if you've gone too far and could upset someone by insisting that they comply with your line of enquiry. Your energy is fluctuating and is not easily stabilised today.

Friday 25th

Going with the flow would be your best stance now. If you're failing to understand the deeper mysteries and nuances of life, step back. You may have a better chance later in the day if you submit to being taught something from the beginning using baby steps.

Saturday 26th

Stick to your core values today as you may be faced with attempting the impossible. However, you could see this as a challenge worth pursuing and get good results. Deviating from the norm would be your best tactic as long as you feel safe and valued. Don't give your services away for free.

Sunday 27th

You might see your inner compass whilst standing in a good place of your own inner strength and compassion. This may be a turning point that guides you closer to your true north and helps you clear space to let in something new. Make use of this great energy.

Monday 28th

Love and relationships may see an upgrade today as you've an emotional attachment to being your best self. Your recent glimpse of this might make you realise how this impacts your work and duties positively. Accept that some things cannot be changed, but you can find room to grow.

MARCH

Tuesday 1st

Radical thinking might help you get to the bottom of a problem at work. Keep chipping away until you make a breakthrough and you could suddenly get your 'aha!' moment. After using a lot of brainpower on this, you may wish to kick back and switch off this evening.

Wednesday 2nd

Today might be destabilising, but in a nice way. If you allow yourself to accept a flow of big and unexpected emotions, you may reach a new level of understanding yourself. A new moon is the green light you need to explore the depths of your own psyche and attain fulfilment.

Thursday 3rd

You may see many things beginning, ending or transforming around you. This is a great time to review your daily schedule and drop everything that is no longer serving your best interests. Today you could be closer to your true values, hopes and dreams than you think. Stay alert.

Friday 4th

An outgoing and positive mood can fuel your day. You might have noticed a shift in your awareness that tells you that there is a big world out there waiting for you to explore. Plan trips or holidays now as your mindset is aligned with what you really need to grow.

Saturday 5th

Listen to elders or people who have experience and wisdom to share. A set of rules and boundaries need to be in place so that everyone knows their place. This may seem frustrating but can be a useful place to start a new cycle. Partners may be extra supportive now.

Sunday 6th

Prepare for an upgrade in your relationships as Venus and Mars enter this area together. Solidarity and quality experiences will enhance your lives. You may also choose to do something for the collective or work for a good cause together. Compassionate warrior energy may be combined and strengthened with love and action.

Monday 7th

Itchy feet or a restless mind helps you to problem-solve or find ingenious ways of working now. Going with the flow or the general vibe might seem like going against your nature and you may try to break out on your own. You must be a team player today.

Tuesday 8th

An emotional pull towards a desired future could be your driving force today. You have a better idea of what you want now and may make plans to achieve this with proper background knowledge. Get in touch with your social and interest groups and start gathering resources from your closest allies.

Wednesday 9th

All the focus today is on your most important relationship. Two minds may be thinking as one and brainstorming ideas that can bear fruit. You could factor in some of your dreams and visions, but be realistic and know that there are certain steps you must take for these to materialise.

Thursday 10th

You may have a lot of thoughts to filter today and these need a logical and rational approach. Put your higher dreams to one side and work out what is necessary and what isn't. If you need help, you would be advised to ask for it from wise and educated friends and elders.

Friday 11th

Give your mind a break today and see to your bodily and spiritual needs. Plan for a weekend of good food and company, or anything else that makes you feel nourished and nurtured. Maternal figures may be supportive. Try going back to something you enjoyed as a child.

Saturday 12th

A day of quality and delightful interactions may feed your soul today. You could be childlike and go on a mini adventure. Think outside the box and spend the day doing unusual things or activities you wouldn't normally have time for. Recharge your batteries by going with the flow.

Sunday 13th

Your true north may be staring you in the face today, but you could be intimidated by it. Maybe you're not ready for the challenge. Maybe this is just a mood that will pass soon. Self-doubt may creep into your awareness. This is your edge; without the irritation, it won't grow.

Monday 14th

You could be extra defensive today but come across as bossy, opinionated and self-righteous. This may be your vulnerable shadow material being projected outside yourself. Recognise what you're doing and what may have triggered it. Don't throw blame around when this could be coming from within you.

Tuesday 15th

Challenges persist and you might not be dealing with them very well. Lie low today and do the responsible thing. Ensure that all your duties and obligations have been met then rest. Stand outside yourself and observe your recent responses and reactions. There may be underlying reasons for poor behaviour from all quarters.

Wednesday 16th

Today you must deal with your immediate surroundings. A decluttering of sorts may help you organise your home and finances, as well as take your mind off personal troubles. Look at ways of keeping a healthy home and mind and this might enhance your feelings of self-worth. A beauty or spiritual treatment may help.

Thursday 17th

Emotions may fluctuate today and cause some inner tension. It would be advisable to work things through in a methodical manner. Finding answers to deeper issues may be easier now if you have a practical mindset. Don't take on anything too big and daunting as it could knock you off course.

Friday 18th

A full moon might highlight issues that need to be cleared out once and for all. You may have come to terms with how you are prone to self-sacrifice in order to have the home you want. You'll be more stable if you get rid of unnecessary baggage.

Saturday 19th

Your mental faculties are a hive of activity today and your curious mind can reconcile difficult facts. A partner may be of use here, but you may struggle to accept their opinion at first. It would be best if you acknowledge that sometimes you need guidance and can't figure out everything by yourself.

Sunday 20th

The spring equinox arrives, and you might be impatient to start a new project or go travelling. This can bring intense feelings. You may desire to get to the root of a few issues within the family and you could be playing detective. Watch that you don't overstep boundaries.

Monday 21st

Spiritual matters can attract you now and you could be making copious enquiries. This could be a journey of self-discovery for you. However, you may not wish to share this with a partner just yet and you might have inner conflict. Go with what your heart is saying.

Tuesday 22nd

Today you might be fixated on things that are ethereal and intangible. If this appears as a valuable path to go down, and it aligns with your core values then pursue it. This evening you may get creative and find ways to expand your horizons without disturbing the peace.

Wednesday 23rd

An emotional attachment to your personal journey may become more important to you now. Your inner voice and compass both have you enraptured, and your mind may be doing overtime. It's possible that you have found a way to shine a light in the outside world. This will fill you with well-deserved satisfaction.

Thursday 24th

Today you could have some moments of doubt and think that you aren't good enough or don't have what it takes to go on a new journey of self-discovery. This mood will pass soon. Concentrate on your mundane duties and return to this issue with a game plan in mind.

Friday 25th

An earthy, grounded, practical activity can be good for you today. You might see a summit ahead and make all the necessary plans to surmount it. You must realise that this isn't a quick fix and will require dedication and innovation. You may be attempting something completely new to you.

Saturday 26th

Using your skillset, devise the steps you must take in a logical order. You might first have to lose some dead weight that has been dragging you down for some time. This could be an attitude or old habit that once helped you to cope but is now immature and unhelpful.

Sunday 27th

Prepare for things to happen fairly quickly now as you have stepped over the brink and committed to a new journey. Your inner critic may have something to say, but you should learn to ignore it and find yourself a cheerleader instead. Look for support in a partner or close friend.

Monday 28th

This is a great day for being brave and compassionate. You might find a guide for your personal journey and understand completely what your limits are. This can be humbling as it isn't a natural default for you. Boundaries will be a big lesson for you later this year.

Tuesday 29th

A dreamy day with nice energy allows you to picture your future self and spurs you on. Spiritual groups may attract you now and can give you a new vision quest or the tools with which to craft your journey. Be flexible and willing to listen to advice from the collective.

Wednesday 30th

Your heart could be expanding today with love for the wider world and humanity. Make sure that you are being authentic now as superficial acts of compassion will be futile. Grab hold of your inner compass and check that it still feels right for you. If it doesn't, then it isn't.

Thursday 31st

You may be all fired up and raring to go today. The trick is to plan well and thoroughly. Acting on impulses might set you back and cost you time. Remember that you're dedicating yourself to a long journey and prepare for the long haul. Travel lightly with an open mind.

APRIL

Friday 1st

This is a great day to set intentions about new starts and adventure. A new moon gives you a signal and asks you to get ready for the road ahead. You could be passionate and eager to begin this new cycle. Your head and heart are in sync.

Saturday 2nd

A map and guidebook might come in handy today. You mustn't run before you can walk. Take time to review the new territory and do a risk assessment. When you're satisfied, you may start putting down roots. Watch how these roots spread through your career prospects.

Sunday 3rd

Listen to your intuition today. You could be restless and pacing around, but you must try to be calm and turn within. It might be useful if you listen to dream messages or long distant connections. This is not the time to act as you're testing the road ahead and scanning for possible obstructions.

Monday 4th

It might be difficult to concentrate on your work duties today as your mind is elsewhere. This may be frustrating, and you could begin to doubt your ability again. Be good to yourself and know that this poor energy will pass soon. Occupy yourself with practical activities or physical exercise.

Tuesday 5th

Your relationship area is where you may see conflicting energy imposing on you. A need to move contrasts with a need to stay within your personal boundaries. This might impact on a lover or partner who may sense that they aren't a priority for you right now. You could notice a disconnect.

Wednesday 6th

Social and interest groups can be supportive and offer you the encouragement you need. You might learn much today if you can put ego aside and accept that some people know more than you. Educate yourself from other people's experiences as there's no point reinventing the wheel.

Thursday 7th

Tricky planetary energy could feel like a rollercoaster today. Your moods may flow as your mind goes around in circles. This afternoon you might feel the need to rest and be alone. Self-care and compassion are important now. Stay in your comfort zone and nourish yourself with whatever makes you feel loved and protected.

Friday 8th

From under your safety blanket, dream big. Allow yourself to envision the best possible version of your life and keep it in your mind's eye. You must take a leap of faith and trust that the universe wants only the best for you. Stay alert to any signs and keep an open mind.

Saturday 9th

Dreamy, floaty energy can carry you away to a fantasy island. Be careful not to get sucked into anything addictive or unreal. Don't stay too long under your blanket as you might find it too comfortable. It may lull you into a false sense of security and give you false hopes.

Sunday 10th

Your self-control returns and you can face the world with a roar. Get ready to express yourself and be authentic, but remember to be honest, kind and respectful. You might cause unnecessary conflict if you speak out of turn and this may set you back a few steps.

Monday 11th

Your career zone could now be filled with research, networking and new concepts to grasp. You might resist this at first. Something may get out of hand today or you could be caught up in your own dreams. You may be at risk of overinflating your ego and becoming a bore.

Tuesday 12th

The day begins with a sense of blockages and restrictions on your progress. You could resort to dreaming and being unrealistic in an attempt to solve problems. This afternoon it eases, and you can make some headway. Learn to separate real from fantasy, and don't allow yourself to fall into unhealthy spirals or thought patterns.

Wednesday 13th

Check your finances today. You might find that you've recently overspent on an indulgent purchase and that recklessness has now come back to bite you. Thorough housekeeping or detoxing bad habits would help to bring you clarity. Clear space both in your home and your mind to keep them healthy.

Thursday 14th

Is there anything you have overlooked regarding your intimate relationships? You might need a last-minute push to get something completed or you could make a rash move and end a partnership. You may need to let off steam somehow and could feel tempted to return to dreams or unhealthy habits to help you cope. A close friend can support you.

Friday 15th

Your thoughts may turn to spiritual matters and the big questions such as why am I here, what is the meaning of life and how do I connect. Be incredibly careful as this could lead you on a downward spiral if you don't have an experienced guide to go through these questions with you.

Saturday 16th

There is a full moon today, which may enhance your communications. It could be that you're filtering fact from fiction and have achieved a good balance of what you know, and what you need to know next. This may give you a good sense of equilibrium and satisfaction.

Sunday 17th

Family matters need your attention today. You could be involved in a group project where your detective-like skills are needed. There may be a little friction, but this can act as a catalyst and force you to see something through from the beginning, right to the end. Use perception and see the wider picture.

Monday 18th

Heavy energy can make an intense start to the week. Try to filter what you say at work as unwanted information can cause tension. You may experience a swing between what you desire and what needs to be changed. Something has to give today.

Tuesday 19th

Creative and romantic pursuits could pass you by today. However much you push, you might not get the answers you require. It could be that you're stretching your wings and getting to know what makes you, or someone else tick, but you're not receiving much clarity or making any progress.

Wednesday 20th

Keep your mind on task today and put your dreams to one side. You could be observed by an elder or a person in authority and will need to make a good impression. This may go against your core values but is necessary in the workplace. Settle down and get things done.

Thursday 21st

You could have a better sense of following guidelines and taking a known route today. Stay flexible and open to instruction. If it seems overwhelming, break it down into bite-size pieces and tackle one at a time. Take your time and remember not to run before you can walk.

Friday 22nd

There is better energy for you to access now and you could come to realise that recent efforts have been rewarded and are in your best interests. You might be more willing to listen or do your research. This may pleasantly surprise those who matter and will be noted.

Saturday 23rd

One-to-one relationships are the focus for the weekend. A stubborn attitude might not get you anywhere if you want your own way. Shared values can be discussed and bring you closer together, but you may need to accept a few home truths now. Talk about your desires and needs.

Sunday 24th

Disruptions in your relationship might cause tension today. You may feel tempted to overstep personal boundaries or even try to manipulate someone. Resist this temptation. Instead, keep communication channels open and stay aware of what is going on with each other.

Monday 25th

Your inner compass may have a little talk with your inner critic today. You will need to be honest with yourself now. If something feels off, it may not be right for you. You should be concentrating on how you might bring compassion and strength together.

Tuesday 26th

You may be aggressive or assertive now. This can be a good thing if there's something that needs completing but may also be exhausting and upsetting. You could be ready to throw everything up in the air and do things by yourself. Consider this carefully as you may alienate someone.

Wednesday 27th

A change of heart brings lighter energy. You could have more empathy or have seen a different perspective and regret causing a fuss. Your true north beckons and asks that you forgive yourself and those you may think have done you wrong. Accepting this may bring blessings and release.

Thursday 28th

It's possible that you might know now that when under pressure, your best bet is to do a practical activity to occupy yourself. Your mundane duties and career have plenty for you to do. Paying attention to these jobs will calm you and bring your mind back down to earth.

Friday 29th

Pluto turns retrograde today. You could now see a period where you use a filtering process to get rid of what has been dragging you down and stopping your progress. Slow down, turn inwards and do some introspection. The journey has a rest stop for you to deal with this. Use it.

Saturday 30th

A new moon and solar eclipse will open some doors for you at work. Take extra caution now as eclipse energy can be unpredictable and anything it brings can disappear again quickly. Good things are happening in your intimate life, which may involve an increase in finances or a spiritual enhancement.

MAY

Sunday 1st

Restless energy can get you out of bed and ready for a busy day of practical activity. You could be doing DIY or getting a beauty make-over. Your choice of activity may be hurried, so watch out for accidents or mistakes. Tasks that have some significant meaning are also favoured.

Monday 2nd

Your heart could be opened wide this morning as you seek to combine dreams and higher knowledge. An opportunity might arise that you will need to give some considerable thought. This may be the start of an overseas project in which you can express your needs and desires.

Tuesday 3rd

Keep slogging at your tasks today. It may feel like wading through mud and you could be exhausted quickly. Your mental energy may be unfocused while your physical energy is lacking. Ask for support and delegate jobs if you can. Don't be disheartened by this temporary lack of progress.

Wednesday 4th

You may have an urge to break free or work in a radical way. Don't feel that you are obliged to make up for lost time. This might bring you some resentment and you may have to fight your corner if being blamed or harassed. A gloomy mood could spoil your evening.

Thursday 5th

An issue at work could be exposed or a big breakthrough can occur. If you feel that all eyes are on you, aim to be modest and impress with your natural abilities. You might be extra defensive or protective about something you perceive as your baby. Don't allow others to take the credit.

Friday 6th

Good and lasting connections can be made today if you search your contacts for advice. You might reach an alliance with a member of a social group who can give you encouragement or point you in the right direction to follow some of your goals and desires.

Saturday 7th

Emotions may be high, and you could be sensitive about things that you would prefer to keep private. There might be an urgent issue to deal with or a last-minute bid to book a holiday. The planetary energy is favourable for travel, intimacy and getting things done such as signing a contract.

Sunday 8th

This is a good day for going after what you want, exploring your self-expression and truly feeling your best self. However, by evening, you could still be fired up and not know how to direct your restlessness. A fitness regime might help, or you may be preparing for the working week.

Monday 9th

Prepare for when Mercury retrograde begins tomorrow. You might already be anticipating problems communicating with a partner. Try not to commit to anything, but remember personal boundaries need to be respected at all times. This is not the best time to push forward with your own agenda.

Tuesday 10th

Mercury turns retrograde in your social area. You will need to be extra careful when interacting with groups. You could have a tendency to say what's on your mind before filtering it. Check your finances today and go through any recent bills calmly and methodically; you may spot something amiss or owing to you.

Wednesday 11th

Travel plans might get a boost now, but plan with caution in mind. Impulsive action may be unwise and ruin an otherwise good idea. Itchy feet can be appeased by good research and getting all the facts. A documentary about your desired place of travel may give you a better itinerary.

Thursday 12th

Today you must find a good balance between simple tasks and larger ones. Prioritise by considering deadlines. You might find a friend has a lot of information to impart but no real evidence or back-up. Gossip or blame could be thrown around your close friendship groups. Stay out of what doesn't concern you.

Friday 13th

Put down roots today as they have a real chance of growth. You might have something you wish to do in the workplace and could do well by making preliminary enquiries. Factor this into your future and watch it develop slowly and steadily into something of value for you.

Saturday 14th

Stay alert today as you may learn something to your advantage. This might not be common knowledge at the moment, but file it away in your mind for future use. Use your keen senses to solve a problem within the family or get to the bottom of a dispute.

Sunday 15th

You have the best energy for a day of activity with the family. It could be that you have to rally the troops and show your leadership qualities. Make something happen by suggesting an unusual activity that all can enjoy. Money matters – especially shared finances – might need attention today too.

Monday 16th

A full moon and lunar eclipse may bring something to a head in your family environment. You could see closure or the completion of a group project. Your energy may build towards achieving one or part of your dreams. Keep ignoring any conflict that has nothing to do with you.

Tuesday 17th

Today you could have sufficient energy to maintain a romantic or creative pursuit. Inspiration flows and you might find a muse to broaden your mind and horizons. Big artistic projects have a good chance of becoming successful now. Choose one and put everything you've got into it.

Wednesday 18th

Ensure that you're putting your energy into the right thing today. There's a chance that you might be following a route that doesn't really align with your core values. However, if you've chosen wisely, you may find that you are racing ahead with it. Slow down and enjoy the journey.

Thursday 19th

You must find it within you to dedicate yourself to one project at a time. A work opportunity may come that requires a total rethink of your approach to completing a task. It may seem arduous at first but will pay off if you take it in baby steps and master them all.

Friday 20th

Accept a challenge to transform an old habit or routine today. Switching things up a little or delegating mundane jobs can give you more time to work on this. Partners can be a source of encouragement and inspire you onwards to greater things.

Saturday 21st

Try to be still and listen out for any subliminal messages from your subconscious. There may be a nasty shock to your system to deal with too. Your social groups may be suffering a revolution or parting of ways. Stay out of it and remain a passive observer.

Sunday 22nd

Today you must play by the rules and find it within you to be empathic to others. Put your own needs to one side and acknowledge the role of an important person in your life. There could be cross words here that come from a place of tension or misunderstanding.

Monday 23rd

You could be returning to a past project at work. An old connection might get back in touch or something you overlooked comes back to cause problems. Use your head and figure out a kind, honest and respectful way to deal with this. Use compassion and try not to get aggressive.

Tuesday 24th

Your inner compass beckons you towards it and you might notice that you've become embroiled in an issue that is not aligned to you. An emotional connection could trigger you this evening and cause you a sleepless night. You may need to process this before acting on it.

Wednesday 25th

The energy is great for making headway with travel or higher education plans. You may find that your many ideas are ready to be refined. Find what works and shed things that are more hassle than they're worth. Be forward-thinking and open-minded.

Thursday 26th

Your mind might be doing overtime and a partner or business associate may be feeding you with knowledge or ideas that you find inspirational and exciting. This can help you to realise your limits and put aside fantasy thinking that will be a waste of your time and effort. You could feel good about this.

Friday 27th

You might have mixed feelings today. A new emotional attachment may be the reason. There could be something that you must let go of in order to make space for the new. Aim for quality in any new plans and start putting down roots.

Saturday 28th

Disturbances and changes may make for a busy day, but you are amenable to them and can get on board with exciting energy. Plans for an enhancement in finances and your working life can fill you with anticipation and you may not get much rest this weekend.

Sunday 29th

Your future goals seem more achievable than ever. Do remember that Mercury is still retrograde, so refrain from signing anything or making an official commitment just yet. Self-doubt may creep in, but this is a passing phase and you should ignore your inner critic and find your cheerleader instead, whether this is an inner voice or a close ally.

Monday 30th

A new moon is a great way to start processing all that you already know and researching that which you still need to know. Social groups could come in handy now as there may be an associate who has had a similar experience and can help you filter thoughts into manageable chunks.

Tuesday 31st

Don't be dismayed today if your true north seems a bit off. It may simply be that there are other things to concentrate on such as your relationship or career. You might be tempted to drift into thinking about personal goals when mundane chores are needing your attention.

JUNE

Wednesday 1st

Go within today and search for what your soul needs. A quiet time with low activity and outside disturbances can help you to unwind and look after yourself. Perhaps plan something that involves good food and company, with which you can feel nurtured and loved. Time alone to process your thoughts would also satisfy you.

Thursday 2nd

You might not be able to avoid disruption at work or in the home today, but this can be positive. You may get inspired to switch things up in either area. This can be a welcome change that takes a new and unexpected route but will bring great benefits to you.

Friday 3rd

Mercury goes direct today. Recent tension in your wider groups might dissolve or be transformed in the coming weeks. This can come as a relief to you if you've been struggling with reconciling group values to your own. Stay in control of your emotions and avoid speaking your mind just yet.

Saturday 4th

Saturn turns retrograde today. This heralds a period where your relationship and shadow could meet, and issues will need to be solved. You may need to put another first for a change or evaluate the boundaries that exist between you. Today, however, brings plans for holidays or other pleasures.

Sunday 5th

Your inner rebel shows itself today and you could be attempting to do something unusual for the day. You might want your own way too much and compromise isn't on your radar, which may cause tension in an important relationship. Staying silent isn't your default but could keep the peace.

Monday 6th

Put your mind to practical or mental tasks today. Keep busy with paperwork and get things straight. This is a good day for a clear-out or a check-in with your body and health. Shopping for healthy foods or creating a schedule to enhance your fitness are also favoured today.

Tuesday 7th

Solid and grounding energy can make you a workhorse today. It's possible that you are beginning to assimilate new duties into your working day and your hard work is paying off. Paying attention to detail and trying new skills will make you feel good about yourself and your productivity.

Wednesday 8th

You may feel out of line with your true north or sense that you're drifting. Don't worry too much; this phase will pass. You have the ability to negotiate and network with people today and you may find yourself released from unnecessary duties.

Thursday 9th

Conversations of all kinds may be tricky. Others could backtrack or renege on a promise and this can leave you feeling out of balance. Don't try to argue your case or keep the peace as you may become drained and demotivated. Try again when the energy has settled, and you can reach a compromise.

Friday 10th

You might learn a valuable lesson today regarding relationships and unconditional love. A partner could come across as stubborn or too involved with other things outside of your relationship. It may be difficult to accept that you also need to make changes. Intense feelings might surface by evening. Remember to breathe.

Saturday 11th

Open your heart today and look at what you value. You might wish to rebel against what isn't bringing you joy. This could be your own sense of self-worth that needs confirmation or validation. If you feel like breaking free or being impulsive, think very carefully before making irreversible changes.

Sunday 12th

Today you might have urges to be rash and radical. You may be acting against your own interests to spite or try to teach others something about you. Family life could suffer if you persist in acting like a child. You might speak out of turn today and cause upset in your tribe.

Monday 13th

An urge to explore all options and set wheels in motion can make you more productive and can achieve some goals. There might be a legal issue or some injustice that urges you to be assertive and proactive. You may be expressing things more positively and making waves.

Tuesday 14th

A full moon can highlight creative and romantic endeavours. You can be determined to be authentic in relationships despite any possible outcome. However, this Moon is expansive and truth-seeking, and your heart opens more than usual. Let the love in and give out the same in return.

Wednesday 15th

You could feel irritable today and not fully understand why. Blockages or restrictions could give you a few temporary problems. Sit back and use your knowledge base to observe what is going on here. You may be missing a vital fact that completes the picture. Don't do anything rash and spoil what you have.

Thursday 16th

Be on the lookout for anything that may enhance your self-esteem or status at work. There might be a financial opportunity here that is too good to miss. You may see that duties change and become more pleasurable. Take time to analyse what this could mean for your future.

Friday 17th

You might be more outgoing and willing to be of service to the greater good now. The outside world holds many different attractions for you, and you may be hard pushed to choose just one. Your romance could benefit from a wider perspective or shared values. A new joint venture is possible.

Saturday 18th

The planetary energy is tricky to manage today. You might feel stuck in a place that is getting boring or not evolving quick enough for you. A test of your boundaries and those of another may trigger selfishness or resentment. Thinking time is important now so stop or pause before responding.

Sunday 19th

A love relationship may deepen if you're prepared to discuss difficult subjects together. Your mind might be pre-occupied with things that are bigger than you. Find the pleasure and enjoyment that makes your relationship unique and keep working on that. Be flexible and open to accept a new viewpoint.

Monday 20th

Your inner compass is in sight and you may check to see if you're still aligned. An urgent issue in your social groups can be distracting you, but can also finalise something you've been thinking about. You could be more invested in breaking free from the norm and doing your own thing.

Tuesday 21st

The summer solstice arrives, and this longest day of light and heat may warm up your inner world. It may not seem so dark and elusive now. You could be compiling a list of summer trips or activities, some of which may include your interest groups.

Wednesday 22nd

You're on fire today and can get all your chores done in record time. Travel or higher education may be combined today and give you something to look forward to in the near future. If you find that you're emotionally attached to this, you can go all out to ensure it happens.

Thursday 23rd

Social groups may offer you a busy schedule for the summer. You will need to balance your relationship time with friends time now. Working hard will pay off today and you can allow yourself some relaxation time this evening with good food and company who inspire you.

Friday 24th

That familiar itch to speak out or right a wrong can niggle you today. You may be fit to burst by evening. Find a different way to use this excess energy. Resist the temptation to rebel in the workplace. Instead, use this energy for something you're passionate about.

Saturday 25th

There could be an issue with your relationship that needs ironing out now. This might involve the things you do for quality time. If you push for your own way you will come away disappointed as the other will push straight back. Consider meeting in the middle and staying true to your values.

Sunday 26th

An activity or get together with your wider friendship groups would be good today. You might simply want to engage in chatter or catch up with your like-minded friends. Aim for a pleasant day of light-hearted conversation and you may enjoy a day of merriment and laughter.

Monday 27th

You could be fired up for the working week yet hit a roadblock that derails you. Find a workable solution without losing your temper or getting aggressive with an elder or person in charge. This can be solved without resorting to behaviour that makes you appear childish or selfish.

Tuesday 28th

Neptune turns retrograde today. As your inner compass, this may affect your personal journey. Under this influence, you should assess how far you've come so far and if anything needs adjusting. Your perspective may be slightly off, and you have a chance to tweak that now.

Wednesday 29th

A sensitive new moon allows you to set goals and intentions regarding your inner work. You may feel more defensive of your privacy but resolve to strengthen personal boundaries. Your intuition could be high now and you would be wise to listen to it. Protect and defend your soft centre without becoming shut off. Talk to a close friend.

Thursday 30th

You might be feeling vulnerable today and this may be hard to shake off. Watch out for situations where you're being used or taken for granted. You might witness passive-aggression or subtle manipulation and this may trigger you. Process all of this before responding irresponsibly.

JULY

Friday 1st

The Moon drops into your sign and brings with it positive energy that is sociable and expansive. You may see an increase in activity with your friendships. This is also a good day for expanding your horizons and travelling. If you must stay at home, you could watch documentaries about places in the world that interest you.

Saturday 2nd

Today you could feel somewhat resentful as you have itchy feet and need to go places and see people. As this may not be possible due to mundane obligations, you might get sulky and have a mini tantrum. A social evening may not give you any satisfaction tonight. Keep some space to breathe if you can.

Sunday 3rd

Partnerships may feel like a burden today, but you can shake this feeling off by talking to friends and online groups. You might get a hint that your shadow is at play and you're projecting your grievances onto your dearest. Find it within you to appreciate the unconditional love the two of you have.

Monday 4th

A sense of urgency helps you complete a task or make a booking of some sort. A last-minute holiday deal may become available. Humility is needed today so that you understand how poorly you relate when your own ego isn't being stroked. You will need to self-analyse and apologise.

Tuesday 5th

Keep your mind on what you value and need, and you might find your productivity amps up a new level. You may give yourself a talking to and feel ashamed of recent behaviour. If you experience triggers in your psyche, acknowledge them and make a note that they wish to be healed.

Wednesday 6th

You could have a day where nothing seems to go your way. Conversations may be strained and leave you trying to mediate or reconcile between two different parts of life. It's best not to struggle or push against the flow. Stay flexible and open-minded and you'll find the place you need to be.

Thursday 7th

Give yourself a break today and let your support groups step in and back you up. They can be a source of support, but you will need to discern who is authentic and who is coming along for the ride. Partnerships may be strong if you remember to maintain healthy boundaries between you.

Friday 8th

If something is difficult to change, leave it alone and it will implode on its own. This might involve a family issue and may be a long-standing problem that is now coming to a head. An emotional investment in this could help you to sweet-talk or come to a compromise.

Saturday 9th

You might be using up a lot of mental energy to solve a problem. Ideas may come and go or appear to be too huge for you to get to grips with. You could still be feeling intense emotions and experiencing triggers from your childhood. Time alone today would be useful.

Sunday 10th

Try not to get too caught up with getting things right at the moment. There may be many changes to deal with and no-one will blame you if you're overwhelmed. Get creative and put feelings down on paper. This can help you to get things straight in your head.

Monday 11th

Self-expression works best when it comes from the heart. You might struggle today as you don't want to offend anyone. However, you may be at your most eloquent now and can put big emotions into words. Just remember to be sincere and honest. Be bold and brave.

Tuesday 12th

Duty calls today and you may be spending most of your time doing mundane jobs for a corporation or business. Do them well as you could be observed by those who have influence. Take small manageable steps and you may achieve a bigger goal than you can imagine. Keep plodding steadily onwards.

Wednesday 13th

A full moon may show you the summit of a very high mountain or the end of a long road. This may be a milestone day for you and will need to be celebrated. Don't let anyone put you down today. You might be triggered and over-sensitive, so stay calm.

Thursday 14th

It's possible that you feel a little lost and confused. This is a passing phase and you could start believing that your personal dreams aren't worth the effort. You may sound off at a partner and this could backfire on you. Use them for support, not a place to vent.

Friday 15th

You could still be feeling challenged or overwhelmed. Irritable energy can make you restless at work and you need an outlet for this. Physical exercise or meditation may help. Don't take out your frustrations on a partner this evening as this will spoil your weekend. Share your feelings respectfully.

Saturday 16th

Your inner world might feel like a tsunami of emotions today. Play your cards right and this may allow you to open up to a partner and reach a new level of understanding. Listen to your intuition as it has good things to say. Triggers are easily dealt with and healed.

Sunday 17th

A change of perspective can be a great help now. You have more self-love and compassion for others. This could continue for some time as it blows away cobwebs from the past and allows you to see the gold or pearls you hide away from others. Friendship groups may offer encouragement and support.

Monday 18th

Find your inner compass and relax into it. You may have noticed that dealing with difficult changes or endings helps you to grow and evolve into your higher self. Self-doubt might creep in, but you manage it better than before. Get active and feel good this afternoon.

Tuesday 19th

Your heart may be expansive, and you could take on duties that serve the greater good. Your inner voice offers you a new mission, so listen carefully. Conversations and networking can be lovely now and you may be doing the research you need for future jobs or interests. Express yourself.

Wednesday 20th

Stick to your guns today. You may be challenged or asked to use up your free time for others. If this doesn't feel good to you, say no and respectfully move on. Things are happening and you need to be on board for them and politely decline trivial obligations for others.

Thursday 21st

Although you have a busy mind, your sense of your own needs is strong. Self-care is more important now. You might be more driven to reach your goals and leave time for yourself this evening. A light turns on in your psyche and you know what's best for you today.

Friday 22nd

Activity at work may be high and goal driven. Envision yourself in the near future and let that be your guide. You might not have time for silly arguments with a partner and may choose to spend an evening by yourself. The Sun enters your sign this evening, Happy birthday!

Saturday 23rd

A social event with friends can be fun and filled with laughter. You could be the centre of attention and step into your normal role, maybe leadership, in your groups. There is a lot of joy to be had today, so connect with those who lift your spirits.

Sunday 24th

You have a lot to give to others now. This might be simply your jovial nature, or you may be hosting a party. Huge intentions and plans make the day exciting, but beware of overdoing the good things. Friendship groups may entice you to burn the candle at both ends.

Monday 25th

Take things slowly today as you could be feeling drained or a bit foggy. You may still be in weekend mode and resist getting down to the daily grind. Take time off this evening to treat yourself to a beauty treatment, good food or an early night.

Tuesday 26th

Instead of getting defensive, respectfully retreat into your own space and take care of your own needs. You could experience criticism and take this very personally. This can turn into poor use of coping mechanisms if you aren't careful. Quiet time can help you process your feelings, which may have become a little over-exaggerated. Take a deep breath and find your centre.

Wednesday 27th

Problem-solving in the workplace comes easily today as you can be more determined and dedicated to your tasks. You may even find an innovative solution that can win you some praise. Maintain a steady pace and you will sail through your duties. Allow yourself some quality time alone to dream this evening.

Thursday 28th

A new moon in your sign is a great time to set goals and intentions regarding your window on the world. You may wish to upgrade your status or take on a new leadership role. Jupiter also turns retrograde and will buy you time if considering travel or higher education.

Friday 29th

Challenging energy can feel as if your plans are all useless and you risk having a tantrum. Take this opportunity to step outside of a situation and view it differently. If nothing succeeds in making you satisfied, leave it and return when the mood has changed.

Saturday 30th

Be careful and mindful of your reactions to a partner. Your mood might be projected onto them and could spoil the weekend. You may inadvertently say what's on your mind without filtering it. Restless feelings require you to do something active. Choose wisely as you could be falling into a trap of your own making.

Sunday 31st

The best thing you can do today is to get out and do some physical exercise alone. It's also a good day for cleaning, decluttering and sorting out any paperwork. Put your mind and body to practical tasks and shake off your poor mood and excess energy.

AUGUST

Monday 1st

This is a great day for taking positive steps towards your career goals. You may receive a promotion or find a new route that is exciting and unique. This will surely enhance your self-worth and maybe even your finances. Put any intangible dreams to one side for the moment and use the energy to make your circumstances more grounded and secure.

Tuesday 2nd

You could be flying high today or you may be restless or agitated. This will be in a good way as there are many great things on offer for you now. Networking and casual conversations may feel a little overwhelming, but this is nothing to fear. You're simply on a new learning curve. Keep looking ahead. You're making progress.

Wednesday 3rd

You might have had a sleepless night as your mind goes into overdrive thinking of all the possibilities available to you now. Be patient and take your time exploring your options. Do your best to ignore your inner critic who may try to fill your head with self-doubt. Listen to your intuition and make it work for you, not against you.

Thursday 4th

Today you would be wise to go over paperwork methodically. You have a keen sense of enquiry now and will spot if something needs adjusting. Emotionally, you may have intense feelings that will benefit from a discussion with your family.

Friday 5th

Be flexible today as your mind and mood may be at odds. You could find that you are revisiting the past and experiencing triggers, which can make you fearful of starting something new. Say goodbye to the past and leave it where it belongs unless you have old skills you can resurrect now.

Saturday 6th

You may have a better sense of what it takes to make you love yourself. Although you would prefer to hide your vulnerability from the workplace, your depth of feeling may surface in your mundane chores. You could possibly be ending something before starting a new journey.

Sunday 7th

Fiery energy helps you to pick yourself up and get excited about something that will enhance your sense of security and allow you to manifest a dream or two. However, try not to get too ahead of yourself as there are rules and regulations you need to observe.

Monday 8th

Try to be adaptable today as there could be some teething problems to deal with. This can be frustrating and can make you irritable. You may be tempted to see these blocks as a bad sign and drown in self-pity. Remember that you must walk before you can run.

Tuesday 9th

Don't allow that old devil on your shoulder to make decisions for you today. You could experience passive aggression or an odd grief that something has ended suddenly. If this triggers your insecurities, ask yourself why and resolve to make more effort to pause before responding to negative stimuli.

Wednesday 10th

This is a highly active day with fluctuating energy. Your emotions may waver until you feel that you'd prefer to hide away for the day. Partner time can help to calm you. What can you do to tell yourself that you're worth some good luck and that this is your chance?

Thursday 11th

You might struggle to get your own way. It could also be that you have hit a roadblock and need to find a way around it. Don't exhaust yourself with this issue, go away for a while, then come back and look at it with new eyes.

Friday 12th

Watch that you don't project your shadow side onto a partner now. It might be that what is going on in your mind comes out unfiltered; that may shock someone you're close to. A full moon can magnify this and make you come across as unfeeling or single-minded. Take a moment to reflect.

Saturday 13th

This weekend you could be bringing work home with you. An issue may need to be dealt with urgently that will require negotiating skills or many messages to and fro. As always, read everything carefully and stay alert for loopholes that may cost you further down the line. Don't spend all day on this.

Sunday 14th

You must be flexible today, which could be difficult for you, but this will allow you to be productive and make any necessary changes to work. Keep your eyes on the goalposts and listen out for well-meaning advice. Practical work and physical exercise are best for you today.

Monday 15th

You have a great sense of what is just and fair. By taking this to those in charge, you may iron out problems before they get out of hand. Keep reading the small print. If something seems too good to be true, then it probably is. Look after yourself today.

Tuesday 16th

Take advantage of your high energy and move things along. You could meet someone with whom you have innovative discussions and who can help filter out the bad from the good. Delegate mundane jobs if you need to as you can't be everywhere at once. Others will have to understand.

Wednesday 17th

If you appear to be working harder than usual, stick with it as it will be noted by those in charge. However, you could be resentful that you've had no time for yourself. This may be something as simple as a missed break or a postponed invitation to enjoy yourself.

Thursday 18th

Deadlines could be closing in and need to be met, but not before you come up with a plan. Stay dedicated and do what needs to be done. If something is truly beyond your capabilities, ask for help and advice from those around you. Don't suffer in silence.

Friday 19th

Stubbornness may get some jobs done but not others. It could be that you need to be a little more flexible and look at something from a different perspective. Changes or endings can feel good today, even if they seem scary at first. Letting go can bring space for something new.

Saturday 20th

Invitations from friends can be enticing. Consider them and allow yourself some fun time. There may be a lot of activity going on within your social groups and this can lift you up and get your busy mind working. Relaxation time will be good for you today. You must remember to laugh.

Sunday 21st

Be mindful of your conversations today. It's possible that you can be boastful or have one drink too many and become unrealistic. Watch your words as you could get into trouble with your friendship groups. Alternatively, you may choose to spend time alone with your thoughts and dreams.

Monday 22nd

Private matters may consume you and you might wish to retreat from hostile situations. Express yourself clearly now and let others know if you need alone time. It may be that you are working through a legal issue or need to catch up with some study. Research is favoured for today.

Tuesday 23rd

This is a great day for checking your finances and duties. You might choose to make beautiful changes in your home, but be warned that this could lead to an expensive impulse buy of something that you don't really need. If it brings you joy, buy it. If it breaks the bank, don't.

Wednesday 24th

Uranus turns retrograde today, and this can be a time of reinventing your ways of working. You might become more radical, but this may also cause you some friction. It's likely that you feel the need to defend your passions and stick to your guns. Maybe more information is needed.

Thursday 25th

A final clear out of files, records or other clutter would be good. You can be most productive if you look at what is holding you back and this may simply be a messy corner you need to deal with. Freshen up your home environment or buy yourself some nice stationery.

Friday 26th

Personal satisfaction comes from getting your own needs met. You may decide to spend a day on beauty treatment or cooking the meals you love. You must attend to your duties before you can indulge yourself as you may be somewhat selfish today.

Saturday 27th

A new moon is the sign you need to make things perfect in your home and finances. A day spent cleaning or on DIY can be pleasing. This can also set the scene for days to come where you may need a clear space in order to get a clear mind.

Sunday 28th

A partner may be moaning about your lack of attention. If you can show that you are busy with home or self-improvements, they will come around. You might have another day of being ruthless and binning useless things that take up too much of your time and energy.

Monday 29th

It's easy for you to switch into work mode today. Your heart and mind are in sync and you may be more goal-driven than usual. Finding a nice home and work balance can bring you pleasure and make you feel good about yourself. You could feel calmer when occupied.

Tuesday 30th

Bring conversations closer to home today. You might need to run around doing small jobs for others or find yourself busy within your community. This could distract you from bigger things and you could feel resentful. Do your chores and allow yourself some you-time this evening.

Wednesday 31st

Your mind could be extra busy now and you might find that you're working on problem after problem. It may not matter whether you succeed in solving them all; what matters is that you are learning to work by the book and not with your own agenda. Be detective-like and consider all avenues.

SEPTEMBER

Thursday 1st

Thinking back to past times could bring nostalgia laced with sadness. You may have bittersweet memories and dwell on these today. There could be a window that needs to be closed once and for all. Turn your mind to whatever brings you joy and quality in your current life.

Friday 2nd

Negative thoughts may linger and have an impact on your relationships with family members and lovers. You might have difficulty getting through the day without some angst today. Communications might be frustrating and you may find your enquiries getting blocked. Don't push unless you're ready to hear some harsh truths.

Saturday 3rd

Fill your weekend with romance and creativity. Thoughts may be put on paper or expressed with eloquence. Watch out for your rising passion that could escalate an ongoing dispute between friends. You might be forcing an issue that isn't quite as important as you think it is.

Sunday 4th

It's crucial that you give yourself forgiveness. You could be reprimanding yourself for arguing with someone you care about. Deep down, your views may not have changed, but you may be willing to reach a compromise and be open and flexible to other perspectives. Be true to yourself and kind to others.

Monday 5th

There might be a long list of chores waiting for you today and you may default to trying to run before you can walk. Research and enquiry can fill your time and you could feel as if you're getting nowhere fast. This may be frustrating, so give yourself extra time to complete each task.

Tuesday 6th

You will access better energy if you keep focused and grounded. You'll have a better sense of what is important and feel drawn to making good impressions. Detective-like skills may be useful this evening as you get to the bottom of an issue or mystery.

Wednesday 7th

Open your heart and feel yourself roar. You may be more uplifted and wish to connect positively with groups and partners. Mentally, you are on top of the world and willing to embrace the people around you. Enjoy reaching out to others simply for the joy of friendship today.

Thursday 8th

Listen to your elders as you could have a lesson to learn about being radical in conventional settings. A partner may show you the benefit of this and encourage and support you with speaking your truth. Know your limits today and try not to overstep personal boundaries or push for answers.

Friday 9th

Today you might find yourself drifting off into a fantasy world. Be careful that this isn't an avoidance tactic you're using to ignore dealing with facts. If you wish to enhance your finances, check your spending and keep hold of receipts.

Saturday 10th

The floaty sensation continues under a full moon and another Mercury retrograde. Be mindful in conversation as you could be floating too far away from reality. This may feel nice, but be careful not to lose your grip or your integrity.

Sunday 11th

Turn your mind towards dreams and visions that have more chance of manifesting. Travel or higher education seem like worthwhile goals for you now. Take your time and do your research. Documentaries about different cultures may satisfy you. Mind how you speak this evening as you are likely to be rather assertive.

Monday 12th

You might wish to do something for the greater good today. A plan may be made to get together with friends for a worthy cause. A partner may appreciate more of your attention this evening; give it unconditionally if you can. Alternatively, it may be you who is seeking more from them.

Tuesday 13th

Spend time on practical tasks and planting seeds for future use. Your personal growth is like a garden that needs tending and today you should do some weeding. Find something old that you can transform or release from your life. Clear space for strong roots and healthy shoots.

Wednesday 14th

Keep your eyes and ears open today as there may be a moneymaking opportunity presented to you. You could also be in the enviable position of bringing more quality to your life. However, refrain from signing any commitments until Mercury is direct again, as more details may be revealed later on.

Thursday 15th

When you put your mind to it, you have a keen sense of what might enhance your immediate environment. Physical activity can help you think and allow you to get clarity. When you see how productive you can be when focused, everything else falls into place and you can relax.

Friday 16th

Stay alert today and look out for any possible tension brewing within your interest groups. Conversations may be misunderstood, or gossip could be rife. If it doesn't concern you, keep out of it. You may be tempted to have your say, but this could make things worse for all involved.

Saturday 17th

You could experience a battle of two greatly opposing opinions. You might feel that this doesn't align with your ideal vision but can't think how to manage it. Let it go over your head and not bother you. If it isn't personal there's no need to get stressed.

Sunday 18th

A quiet day of contemplation and introspection may be the best way to spend your time now. You might be feeling defensive and protective, and recent events could have triggered old feelings and habits. An injustice may get to you that you have to keep to yourself for now. All things have their time.

Monday 19th

Go easy on yourself today and try not to get side-tracked by anything outside your work. You could gain some satisfaction from looking after number one and enjoying the safety of your own home. Find the pleasure in simple things and give gratitude for what you have.

Tuesday 20th

Subtle manipulation can force you out of hiding this afternoon. If this is because you need to stand up for yourself, make sure that you're ready to confront a few deep-seated fears and anxieties. This could be a day of strength if you handle this in a mature and responsible manner.

Wednesday 21st

You could be feeling emotional about things you perceive as unfair today. If you have trouble in conversations and can't make yourself heard, shouting about it will make it worse. Accept that this is a minor phase that will pass soon enough. Keep your mood upbeat with research and study.

Thursday 22nd

Your shadow may come out to play now and you may feel stuck and blocked. Find an outlet that allows you to let off steam healthily. Your workplace and relationships will come under fire if you can't get rid of irritation or anxiety. Do something just for you this evening.

Friday 23rd

Be still and silent. Your subconscious might have something to tell you. Messages or symbols may give you a clue on how to proceed with your day. Your home may benefit from decluttering, which can help to give you a clear mind. Check on your health and diet too.

Saturday 24th

You may want to avoid dealing with your current issues by relying on unhealthy coping mechanisms today. Think positive and aim for fresh and good things that you can incorporate into your everyday lifestyle. Friends and interest groups may add to your anxiety; if you feel that way, politely decline invitations and stay in your own home this evening.

Sunday 25th

Today can be tricky as your emotions may fluctuate greatly. Try to find what adds quality to your life and add more of that. A new moon is a great time to set intentions around achieving a good balance between different parts of life, most importantly, significant relationships and partnerships.

Monday 26th

Listen to your self-talk now. You may have two conflicting voices causing some confusion. Something has to change today or at the very least, be transformed into something more useful. Legal issues and other money matters may surface to be dealt with. Check that all is fair and just.

Tuesday 27th

There could be a forced change that is out of your control. You may turn to friends or lovers to help with this but ultimately, it's something you need to deal with alone. When you can accept that this is necessary for your personal growth, you can relax and anticipate better times.

Wednesday 28th

Listen to your elders today. You could receive good advice and wisdom from those who have experienced something similar to what you're going through. Plan to spend more time on your body's needs. A regular exercise or meditation routine would be good for you and help get rid of excess energy.

Thursday 29th

Issues from the past can come back to trouble you. You could be holding onto a view or habit that is detrimental to your overall health. Intense feelings such as jealousy or old grievances within the family may bother you. Re-align with your inner compass and your personal values, and consider how far forwards you've come.

Friday 30th

There is better energy today and you might feel creative, romantic or playful. You can be more adventurous and possibly plan for an exciting trip away. Eating well and enjoying good company can lift your spirits and inspire you to get out of a rut that is going nowhere.

OCTOBER

Saturday 1st

Try not to barge through a partner's boundaries today. It's likely that you're optimistic and joyful, but remember that your significant other might not feel the same way. This can make it difficult to feel closeness. You may need to be flexible or accommodating until they're ready to join in your joy.

Sunday 2nd

Mercury turns direct now. You may experience a fog beginning to lift from your true north, but you must be cautious as there may still be an illusion underneath. There's little point starting something new today as the energy suggests that you could lose interest in it very quickly.

Monday 3rd

Watch out for opportunities at work that can enhance your finances or make more sense of your personal growth. Offers from earlier in the year may be up for review. Is there anything you can offer to tailor this experience to suit you better? Can you put your own spin on it?

Tuesday 4th

This morning you would be wise to use practical skills and ensure you get noticed. As the day progresses, so might your visibility to those who matter. Mental activity can take over and you may be networking or gathering resources and allies for a future exciting project.

Wednesday 5th

You may feel a little stuck today but there is a chance you can work around this by thinking outside the box. Be prepared to take on board the advice of others. Don't dismiss anything until you've had time to look at it and see if it could work for you.

Thursday 6th

Merging with like-minded people or getting lost in love can take you to ethereal and magical places, but you will need to keep one foot on planet Earth. You can succumb temptations, including romance now. You may upgrade your relationships by combining forces instead of fighting from opposite corners.

Friday 7th

Listen to your inner voice today as it may tell you what needs to be released or transformed in order to grow. This may be another lesson in starting at the beginning and not jumping straight into the middle. Your intuition will guide you, so stay alert for subliminal messages and signposts.

Saturday 8th

Hold onto your true north now and let that be your anchor. You could feel pulled in directions that don't feel safe or true. Don't do anything rash today as it may get out of hand and return to bite you. Make sure that any new plans for travel are realistic.

Sunday 9th

A full moon can throw the spotlight on travel and education plans. It might also reflect on your actions for the last six months. You may see something come to fruition now. Pluto turns direct and may also bring about an ending concerning mundane work duties and health.

Monday 10th

You could be more outgoing today and wish that you'd taken up invitations at the weekend. This might mean that you play catch up with your social network. Be your best self in the workplace today. Your leadership skills may be needed to organise new projects or discard old ones.

Tuesday 11th

Negotiation might become a theme for you in the next few weeks. This could come naturally to you as you can converse with a persuasive style. You may recall skills learned when needing to get your own way, but you have also developed a mature listening style too.

Wednesday 12th

Tricky planetary energy may give you a roller-coaster of a day. You might think you're winning one minute and see it all fall apart the next. Deal with this by removing any expectations for outcomes beyond your control. Changes will come whether you want it or not. Be practical and stay grounded.

Thursday 13th

You might wish to seek advice from interest groups today. There could be someone within them who has wisdom to share. An issue of justice could stop you in your tracks, but you may be more prone to sit up and listen to the whole story and not just one side.

Friday 14th

You have more time for others today and can be unusually altruistic and patient. A good cause may have touched a soft spot in you, and you now wish to offer your services. Know your place with this and learn all about it before committing on a whim.

Saturday 15th

You have two choices on how to spend your weekend. You might either retreat and be alone with your private thoughts or you could be defensive on behalf of others. You may feel part of something big and wish to add your voice to a caring and nurturing cause.

Sunday 16th

If your emotions are activated, make sure they are in sync with your mind. You could be over-sensitive towards something that you haven't fully thought through. Make sure that you have all the facts before making an emotional decision you may need to undo at a later date.

Monday 17th

You could become entangled in a web of misunderstanding and wrong action today. You may think that you're doing the right thing but could also feel manipulated or coerced. Don't commit to anything that will become a burden. If you can get out of it, do so politely and put it down to a lesson learned.

Tuesday 18th

The Moon drops into your sign and you may find your own voice and self-expression. You could be shouting about recent events or making a scene. Try not to get above yourself now. If this was an injustice against you personally, feel free to question it.

Wednesday 19th

If you must make noises today, draw on the archetype of the compassionate warrior. There are ways of dealing with unrest that don't need to be aggressive. Be respectful and assertive. You may be at risk of raising a revolution in your own backyard, and you could be the only member.

Thursday 20th

Control struggles may surface but the energy suggests that with proper management, you can handle them with reason and strategy. If you can keep emotions out of decision-making, you may get somewhere. Spend time this evening going over any paperwork involved in this as you may find the get-out clause you're looking for.

Friday 21st

Today you can look at what holds value for you. What can you not do without? You may be deciding what is worth holding onto and what has been holding you back. This will also include family relationships and work issues. Have a think about what makes you feel good or bad.

Saturday 22nd

There could be a last-minute thing to do concerning messaging or visiting in your locality. This may need to be done in the morning before you are bogged down with other obligations. A day of practical activity may take your mind off other worries that aren't sitting well with you.

Sunday 23rd

Saturn turns direct today and you might be reviewing the subject of boundaries and limits in your significant relationship. If these have been issues for you this year, you may come to an understanding now. Love and seduction may become a theme; make sure it's what you both want.

Monday 24th

You might find that partnerships are on the mend and have developed more trust. With a good balance between you, you can discuss things calmly and equally. Your head and heart are in sync, which is a great starting point for a deep discussion.

Tuesday 25th

A new moon and solar eclipse can open a window of wildcard activity where anything could happen. It's possible that you see issues of jealousy or power struggles arising within your family. However, you may now have the ability and compassion to handle this well and bring about a good outcome.

Wednesday 26th

Try not to resurrect old issues from the past when dealing with family as it may implode on you and be detrimental to your day. Remember what you've learned from Saturn this year and maintain healthy and loving boundaries. This may test your patience, but will win you complete respect.

Thursday 27th

Use your intelligence today before emotions. You might have more luck making changes and setting ground rules if you feel inspired and guided by logic and reason. This afternoon you may take off and soar to higher levels in your romance and creative pursuits. Make the most of this energy.

Friday 28th

You could be revisiting an experience that is fathomless and spiritual. This may be with a partner or a group and you could be once again on cloud nine. Make sure that this isn't anything superficial. Keep it real by anchoring yourself to your love.

Saturday 29th

If you wake to feel drained, choose to stay cosy and quiet with a loved one. Shared duties and intense conversations may bring the two of you even closer together. Cooking, eating or doing mundane chores can be a delight now if you have someone to share them with. Prepare for conversations to get juicy.

Sunday 30th

Mars turns retrograde today. This can herald a time of turbulence and blocks within friendship groups. Social interactions might reach a stalemate situation where no side will move. However, for today, you may enjoy a time of sweet mystery and depth in your family of origin.

Monday 31st

Stay in control of your feelings today as the working week may dampen your good spirits. Don't be tempted to raise a revolution. You might have cross words in your family that risk getting nasty. Rise above it and be respectful and mature. This will pass and be soon forgotten about.

NOVEMBER

Tuesday 1st

You may be presented with several challenges today that bring out your shadow side. Your emotions might be on edge and any little thing will trigger an adverse reaction. Understand that this is temporary and keep a low profile. Don't provoke an argument as you may not win.

Wednesday 2nd

Take things slowly today as your mental energy may be overloaded or blocked. You might see confusion or aggression within your friendship groups or close relationships. This evening may be lighter if you stay adaptable and willing to let go of old grievances. It's time to heal old wounds.

Thursday 3rd

Your sense of empathy is strengthened now, and you could be fixing problems with family members. Humble yourself to apologise and enter into negotiations with more compassion. This will help to make you feel connected not only by blood but by love and spirit. Merging with your soul group can be soothing now.

Friday 4th

A change of direction may still be uncomfortable, but you might realise that it will feel right for you eventually. Issues within your social groups need to be avoided, not antagonised. Serving others with unconditional love can fill your heart and bring you more joy and optimism.

Saturday 5th

You can be more outgoing and have more passion for your dreams and intentions. This can mean that you are also seeing clearly where you have been held back with karmic connections. These ties must be cut now and release you from their bonds. You might do this suddenly and with total conviction.

Sunday 6th

A conflict could arise that is simply about spending time with a lover or with friends. Choose wisely as you may resent your time being wasted by one party. Your inner voice will remind you of what you've let go recently, but will also give you encouragement and confidence to move on.

Monday 7th

You might have a better mood today, although you could be a little stubborn. Small annoyances with family and lovers may test your patience and you will need to remember your personal boundaries. You might need to balance home life with the work you do for the wider world.

Tuesday 8th

A full moon and lunar eclipse can show the closure of a recent episode. A project may be completed and ready to move to the next level. There is anticipation in the air, and you could find it hard to stay still and keep quiet. Something wonderful is ready to burst into life.

Wednesday 9th

You can be very social today, but may also be at risk of revealing a secret or speaking too soon. Tread carefully today as there could be a lot depending on a certain issue. You may need to hold your tongue a little longer. This might be tricky.

Thursday 10th

Be cautious and know where your limits are. This is a crucial time, and you don't want to spoil it by being reckless. A big dream may be coming true and you may not want the bubble to burst. Your emotions may be intense but can be shared.

Friday 11th

It might be tricky to follow your head as you're emotionally invested in doing the right thing. You could be dragged into a problem with your social groups that may go against your core values. If this doesn't seem fair or just to you, walk away.

Saturday 12th

Have time alone and nurture yourself with what makes you feel good. Great company, especially maternal figures can be soothing and remind you that you're loved. Listen to your intuition today as there may be mysteries unravelling that you now have more understanding of. Don't let anyone fool you with false promises.

Sunday 13th

You might be building your comfort zone around you and inviting in those who you feel safe with. This may be an exclusive set of people from your family who are on your wavelength. Enjoy the emotions you feel today and let them guide you towards setting a better course.

Monday 14th

Stay in control today and try not to react if someone pushes your buttons, you could experience a small trigger but can deal with it admirably. This afternoon it is safe to emerge and let your voice be heard. You may shine your light and attract others to it.

Tuesday 15th

An act of compassion can go a long way. Your family may need reassurance or legal advice. You might be the one to deal with communication and enquiries. An investment may pay off or other money matters could come to a head and need attention.

Wednesday 16th

Fight for your rights today, but remember to do so with total honesty. Look out for dishonest dealings that could affect you or your family. This may be a trickster or perhaps simply some energy that is elusive and not clear. You might uncover a falsehood and see the truth behind the lies.

Thursday 17th

Check all the facts today, then check them again. This is a good day to go through your paperwork and finances. Mercury joins Venus in your romantic and creative zone, and you could be more articulate with words of love. Let them flow from your wide-open heart.

Friday 18th

Restlessness can be the fuel you need to get your work done today. You could be fine-tuning some details and using radical methods to solve problems. Focus on practical work and you might get much done in record time. Avoid any conflict or slow progress within your social groups.

Saturday 19th

Today you may have a good feeling that all is well in the world. You manage to separate from the problems of others and concentrate on what means the most to you. A healthy regard for a romantic partner can inspire you to create beauty and have heartfelt conversations.

Sunday 20th

Your mind is busy processing a lot of ideas that pertain to your love relationship. An understanding might have been reached that is both respectful and mature. You may have found a better sense of boundaries and limits, and find that you have no intention of breaching those or risking what you have with someone you love.

Monday 21st

You might need to add a finishing touch to an issue within your family group. This will involve some difficult emotions as you could be finalising a deal or letting something go. Let your tribe know that you're there to share this moment with them. Your love life may be filled with blessings this evening.

Tuesday 22nd

The Sun enters your romance and creative zone. Expect to be inspired or find your muse. Your greatest work could be born from this energy. Expressing yourself will be easily done as you are more prone to speaking your divine truth and searching for the meaning of life.

Wednesday 23rd

Your emotions may be bigger than usual, and you could be making grand gestures in several parts of your life. You may be skipping through your day like a child filled with joy and optimism for the future. Be careful not to overstretch yourself, but enjoy the remarkable energy.

Thursday 24th

This is a wonderful day, so take note of what occurs. A new moon asks you to set goals and intentions regarding your romance, creativity and search for truth and wisdom. Meanwhile, your heart is totally in sync with your head and love is in the air, filling your lungs.

Friday 25th

Don't let anyone knock you from your happy spot. You might need to deal with difficult people who put a downer on your day. This could be a person who simply dislikes another person enjoying some fortune and happiness. Deal with them respectfully and compassionately.

Saturday 26th

Simple pleasures can bring the most smiles. Today you could feel that everything is where it should be and acknowledge that you've done hard work on yourself this year. Maybe a reward or treat is needed. Get your chores done then do something just for you, or share it with a close friend or lover.

Sunday 27th

It is becoming clearer to you that your true north has moved away from where it once was. You might notice that what was once important, no longer is. Your experiences and fortunes this year may have shifted your value system and you may be looking at a healthier, less cluttered path.

Monday 28th

You can be more open to helping a cause or doing good work in your community now. There may be a way you can make positive change happen with a new group of like-minded people. You could try enticing your other social groups to get on board and participate.

Tuesday 29th

A partner may get all your mental attention today. You could be bouncing through your day with thoughts of love and closeness spurring you on. Remember to come back down to earth and get your regular chores done. Stay away from argumentative or antagonistic groups this evening.

Wednesday 30th

Keep a grip on reality, as you're in danger of drifting off to a fantasy island. Consider what depths you will go to for someone you love. Would they return the favour? If you mean to share everything with them, make sure that the feeling is mutual. Do this through honest, open and loving communication.

DECEMBER

Thursday 1st

It's possible that you hit a snag today and may be coerced into something you don't wish to do. If it feels wrong and not in alignment with your best interests, walk away from it. This is your inner compass keeping you on the straight and narrow. Stay closer to home for now.

Friday 2nd

Your keen sense of what is right and just can help you avoid unnecessary conflict. A partner may offer the support you need if you are unsure. Set your sight on what will bring you security; this may mean ignoring the impulse to go off and do your own thing.

Saturday 3rd

Steering your own boat may feel isolating, but if you know what's good for you, your course will be true. Stay respectful and responsible at all times. Put your energy into what you and you alone feel passionate about and ignore others who may try to draft you to their cause.

Sunday 4th

Neptune turns direct now. Your inner compass is strong and pulls you away from potential trouble. Listen to your inner voice. As always, do practical work to distract yourself from making fiery and impulsive decisions. Stay grounded and keep your mind busy with jobs around your home.

Monday 5th

If you need to shake things up a little today, then do so. It could be that something has lain dormant and has gathered dust. This might be a work issue that is yet to get a breakthrough moment. There is also an urgency to merge or connect with something bigger than yourself.

Tuesday 6th

You need another push to finish a creative project or let someone know how you feel. Put down roots or build solid foundations today, but you can only do this by speaking honestly and staying true to your personal path. You will soon know the steps you need to take.

Wednesday 7th

Use today to gather your thoughts and resources. Thinking time will do you good and help you to process recent events. Social groups of like-minded friends can be encouraging and offer you well-meaning advice. Take it on board and dedicate thinking time to it. Cover all your options.

Thursday 8th

What has come to light within your groups? You might see something exposed or experience aggressive behaviour. Alternatively, you may have reached a stalemate situation and be at a loss how to move on. Keep thinking and explore all open avenues. Don't bother trying to tear down brick walls.

Friday 9th

Retreat into your private zone today and allow yourself to feel safe. You might feel uncertain and prefer to simply be with those who love you unconditionally. You may be sensitive to criticism, so try not to engage or react. Filter your words before speaking them aloud.

Saturday 10th

Stay safe now as you may not be in the right frame of mind to deal with any upsets. Look after your body by eating well. Choose the right company to make you feel more nurtured and protected. You may have a trigger directed at an open wound that still needs healing.

Sunday 11th

Your dreams will tell you where you should be heading, but you could still feel insecure and vulnerable. It may be a case of "too much, too soon". This is a passing phase that is triggering your deepest self. Wait until you have more clarity.

Monday 12th

The Moon is back in your sign and you feel more like yourself again. You might be stirred up with passions and ready for action again. Take this time to pause and reflect before making any moves. Surveying your territory will help you gauge the audience you need to convince.

Tuesday 13th

Be careful that you don't project your shadow side onto a partner. You may find that the strength of your convictions overwhelms you now and you need an outlet. Try using your creative side and self-expression to illustrate how you feel. Be open to any inspiration you may receive.

Wednesday 14th

Get down to the nitty-gritty of the working day. Lists, plans and clearing out can help you to focus. You may also wish to check your health and resolve to start an exercise regime. This may feel like an arduous task, but it will ultimately be positive.

Thursday 15th

Great earth energy can ensure that you get all your jobs done today. You can be more methodical and self-disciplined now. Avoid any distractions from social groups as they won't bring you much joy today. Happiness comes from ticking things off your list and clearing space for new things to come.

Friday 16th

Apply yourself to the job in hand and stay open to any changes you may need to make along the way. By evening, you could have satisfaction from knowing that you've been productive and useful. Your dreams and visions might call, but they must wait for another time.

Saturday 17th

Find time in the day to take care of your own needs. This may simply involve an exercise routine to stretch your body. Planning a tasty evening meal would also be good, especially if this includes a love partner. Food, company and conversation are the themes of the day.

Sunday 18th

You may be tempted to chat the day away, but you might feel guilty doing so. A lover may have something to discuss, but they could also encourage you to work first and play later. This evening is good for a lively conversation between the two of you that can reach new heights.

Monday 19th

Be sincere in the workplace now. There may be a way of offering your services that doesn't overwhelm you with more duties. Family matters can be intense as the festive season rapidly approaches. You might need to make a plan or delegate jobs so that all hands are on deck.

Tuesday 20th

Jupiter returns for a long stay in your travel zone. This is great news as any holidays or interest in other cultures will likely take you far and wide. Try to be flexible and listen to your partner's views on this. You could even make a booking today.

Wednesday 21st

The winter solstice arrives today and brings a long, dark night. This is perfect to snuggle down with a partner and express gratitude for the year gone by. Try to reflect on your personal growth and notice how far you've come. Set wheels in motion for exploring in the new year.

Thursday 22nd

You might wish to do something unusual now. An urge for pleasure, unplanned journeys and a taste of your dreams may fill you. You can do this by food shopping for the coming festivities. The traditional way may not interest you this year, so do something outside the box and have fun.

Friday 23rd

There is a new moon this morning, which may be the first step in a long inner journey. You may take stock of this and think it's too big for you, but remember that you must follow the rules and do things by the book to get where you want to be.

Saturday 24th

Love, merriment and great conversation fill your heart. You might envision yourself walking side by side with the partner of your dreams on the long road to realising your visions and ambitions. You may also be planning this alone and taking into consideration what it means to you.

Sunday 25th

Today is best spent with a partner as your emotions are focused on them. You might also be thinking about the wider world and your small part in it. It could be time to think about offering your services to a good cause and contributing to the world community in some way.

Monday 26th

You could be tired and lacking in energy, but there may still be family obligations to fulfil. The best thing to do today is to be friendly or civil and do your duties to others. You can let them know your limits, as you may well have overdone the good things yesterday.

Tuesday 27th

Let yourself merge with your tribe and switch off for a while. You may desire to indulge in more food and drink and simply relax. If you're on cloud nine, try to keep one foot on the ground and anchor yourself in reality. All feels good and peaceful now.

Wednesday 28th

Keep an eye out for your blessings today. They might come in an unexpected form. Your inner compass is in your grasp and that can be intoxicating. You could feel that you're in an ethereal world where all your dreams will come true. Keep it real and don't get swept away.

Thursday 29th

Before the year ends, Mercury turns retrograde. Prepare for this by backing up all devices and double-checking travel plans. You might notice this influence immediately with plans for health or beauty being disturbed. Be mindful of conversations with a loved one as there may be a misunderstanding. Patience is key.

Friday 30th

A quiet day would be good for you now. You could be missing your friendship groups and wish to get out and about, but there may not be much going on. Don't be dismayed by this; do what you want to do. Make plans for holidays and adventures in the coming year.

Saturday 31st

If you still don't have your celebrations planned, consider staying in your own home and hosting them there. You may feel better if you are in control of the proceedings and the star of your own show. See out the old year in style, and share your joy and optimism with the people you love most. Have a wonderful close to 2022.

Leo

PEOPLE WHO SHARE YOUR SIGN

PEOPLE WHO SHARE YOUR SIGN

....

Leonians have studded the stage, ruled the roost and brought laughter and fun into people's lives for decades. Whether they choose to be actors or are royalty (or, in the case of Meghan Markle, both), Leonians shine in the spotlight. Discover the courageous and sparkling stars who share your exact birthday, and see if you can spot the similarities.

23rd July

Daniel Radcliffe (1989), Paul Wesley (1982), Kathryn Hahn (1973), Monica Lewinsky (1973), Marlon Wayans (1972), Philip Seymour Hoffman (1967), Slash (1965), Woody Harrelson (1961), Jo Brand (1957)

24th July

Turia Pitt (1987), Mara Wilson (1987), Elisabeth Moss (1982), Anna Paquin (1982), Rose Byrne (1979), Danny Dyer (1977), Jennifer Lopez (1969), Kristin Chenoweth (1968), Amelia Earhart (1897), Alexandre Dumas (1802)

25th July

Paulinho (1988), James Lafferty (1985), Shantel VanSanten (1985), D.B. Woodside (1969), Matt LeBlanc (1967), Iman (1955), Estelle Getty (1923), Rosalind Franklin (1920)

26th July

Stormzy (1993), Taylor Momsen (1993), Kate Beckinsale (1973), Jason Statham (1967), Sandra Bullock (1964), Helen Mirren (1945), Mick Jagger (1943), Stanley Kubrick (1928), Aldous Huxley (1894), Carl Jung (1875), George Bernard Shaw (1856)

27th July

Winnie Harlow (1994), Taylor Schilling (1984), Jonathan Rhys Meyers (1977), Tom Kerridge (1973), Maya Rudolph (1972), Nikolaj Coster-Waldau (1970), Triple H (1969), Julian McMahon (1968)

28th July

Harry Kane (1993), Cher Lloyd (1993), Soulja Boy (1990), John David Washington (1984), Alexis Tsipras, Greek Prime Minister (1974), Lori Loughlin (1964), Hugo Chávez, Venezuelan President (1954), Jacqueline Kennedy Onassis (1929)

29th July

Joey Essex (1990), Fernando Alonso (1981), Josh Radnor (1974), Wil Wheaton (1972), Sanjay Dutt (1959), Tim Gunn (1953), Geddy Lee (1953)

30th July

Joey King (1999), Yvonne Strahovski (1982), Jaime Pressly (1977), Hilary Swank (1974), Christine Taylor (1971), Christopher Nolan (1970), Simon Baker (1969), Terry Crews (1968), Lisa Kudrow (1963), Laurence Fishburne (1961), Arnold Schwarzenegger (1947), Henry Ford (1863)

31st July

Victoria Azarenka (1989), B. J. Novak (1979), Emilia Fox (1974), Antonio Conte (1969), J. K. Rowling (1965), Wesley Snipes (1962), Louis de Funès (1914)

1st August

Jack O'Connell (1990), Bastian Schweinsteiger (1984), Jason Momoa (1979), Ryoko Yonekura (1975), Coolio (1963), Yves Saint Laurent (1936), King Abdullah of Saudi Arabia (1924), Herman Melville (1819)

2nd August

Charli XCX (1992), Edward Furlong (1977), Sam Worthington (1976), Kevin Smith (1970), Mary-Louise Parker (1964), Wes Craven (1939), Peter O'Toole (1932), James Baldwin (1924)

3rd August

Karlie Kloss (1992), Charlotte Casiraghi (1986), Evangeline Lilly (1979), Tom Brady (1977), James Hetfield (1963), Martha Stewart (1941), Martin Sheen (1940), Terry Wogan (1938), Tony Bennett (1926)

4th August

Cole and Dylan Sprouse (1992), Crystal Bowersox (1985), Meghan, Duchess of Sussex (1981), Anna Sui (1964), Barack Obama, U.S. President (1961), Billy Bob Thornton (1955), Louis Armstrong (1901), Queen Elizabeth the Queen Mother (1900)

5th August

Olivia Holt (1997), Jesse Williams (1981), James Gunn (1966), Mark Strong (1963), Pete Burns (1959), Maureen McCormick (1956), Neil Armstrong (1930), Joseph Merrick (1862)

6th August

Charlotte McKinney (1993), Ferne McCann (1990), Robin van Persie (1983), Vera Farmiga (1973), Geri Halliwell (1972), Michelle Yeoh (1962), Barbara Windsor (1937), Andy Warhol (1928), Lucille Ball (1911), Alexander Fleming (1881)

7th August

Helen Flanagan (1990), Rick Genest (1985), Abbie Cornish (1982), Charlize Theron (1975), Michael Shannon (1974), David Duchovny (1960), Bruce Dickinson (1958), Wayne Knight (1955)

8th August

Shawn Mendes (1998), Princess Beatrice of York (1988), Roger Federer (1981), Meagan Good (1981), Chris Eubank (1966), The Edge (1961), Dustin Hoffman (1937), Emiliano Zapata (1879)

9th August

Bill Skarsgård (1990), Anna Kendrick (1985), Audrey Tautou (1976), Gillian Anderson (1968), Eric Bana (1968), Whitney Houston (1963), Michael Kors (1959), Melanie Griffith (1957), Jean Piaget (1896)

10th August

Kylie Jenner (1997), Brenton Thwaites (1989), Devon Aoki (1982), JoAnna García (1979), Angie Harmon (1972), Justin Theroux (1971), Suzanne Collins (1962), Antonio Banderas (1960), Juan Manuel Santos, Colombian President (1951), Herbert Hoover, U.S. President (1874)

11th August

Alyson Stoner (1993), Jacqueline Fernandez (1985), Chris Hemsworth (1983), Anna Gunn (1968), Joe Rogan (1967), Viola Davis (1965), Hulk Hogan (1953), Steve Wozniak (1950)

12th August

Cara Delevingne (1992), Mario Balotelli (1990), Tyson Fury (1988), François Hollande, French President (1954), George Soros (1930), Cantinflas (1911), Erwin Schrödinger (1887)

13th August

DeMarcus Cousins (1990), MØ (1988), Sebastian Stan (1982), Alan Shearer (1970), Debi Mazar (1964), John Slattery (1962), Prime Minister of Cuba Fidel Castro (1926), Alfred Hitchcock (1899), Annie Oakley (1860)

14th August

Brianna Hildebrand (1996), Nick Grimshaw (1984), Mila Kunis (1983), Paddy McGuinness (1973), Halle Berry (1966), Emmanuelle Béart (1963), Magic Johnson (1959), Steve Martin (1945), Doc Holliday (1851)

15th August

Jennifer Lawrence (1990), Joe Jonas (1989), Ben Affleck (1972), Anthony Anderson (1970), Debra Messing (1968), Melinda Gates (1964), Alejandro González Iñárritu (1963), Anne, Princess Royal (1950)

16th August

Evanna Lynch (1991), Cam Gigandet (1982), Frankie Boyle (1972), Steve Carell (1962), Madonna (1958), Angela Bassett (1958), James Cameron (1954), Charles Bukowski (1920)

17th August

Taissa Farmiga (1994), Austin Butler (1991), Thierry Henry (1977), Donnie Wahlberg (1969), Helen McCrory (1968), Sean Penn (1960), Robert De Niro (1943), Mae West (1893)

18th August

Maia Mitchell (1993), Frances Bean Cobain (1992), G-Dragon (1988), Andy Samberg (1978), Edward Norton (1969), Christian Slater (1969), Patrick Swayze (1952), Robert Redford (1936)

19th August

Ethan Cutkosky (1999), Christina Perri (1986), Melissa Fumero (1982), Fat Joe (1970), Matthew Perry (1969), John Stamos (1963), Gerald McRaney (1947), Bill Clinton, U.S. President (1946), Gene Roddenberry (1921), Coco Chanel (1883)

20th August

Demi Lovato (1992), Andrew Garfield (1983), Ben Barnes (1981), Amy Adams (1974), Misha Collins (1974), David Walliams (1971), Fred Durst (1970), David O. Russell (1958), Joan Allen (1956), Robert Plant (1948)

21st August

Bo Burnham (1990), Hayden Panettiere (1989), Robert Lewandowski (1988), Usain Bolt (1986), Laura Haddock (1985), Carrie-Anne Moss (1967), Kim Cattrall (1956), Kenny Rogers (1938), Wilt Chamberlain (1936)

22nd August

James Corden (1978), Rodrigo Santoro (1975), Kristen Wiig (1973), Richard Armitage (1971), Adewale Akinnuoye-Agbaje (1967), Ty Burrell (1967), Honor Blackman (1925), Ray Bradbury (1920)

23rd August

Jeremy Lin (1988), Kobe Bryant (1978), Julian Casablancas (1978), Scott Caan (1976), Ray Park (1974), River Phoenix (1970), Rick Springfield (1949), Gene Kelly (1912)